Living Political Ideas

Power, Dissent, Equality: Understanding Contemporary Politics

This book is part of a series produced by Edinburgh University Press in association with The Open University. The complete list of books in the series is as follows:

What is Politics?
Jef Huysmans

Exploring Political Worlds
Edited by Paul Lewis

Politics and Power in the UK
Edited by Richard Heffernan and Grahame Thompson

Living Political Ideas
Edited by Geoff Andrews and Michael Saward

Making Policy, Shaping Lives
Edited by Raia Prokhovnik

The books form part of an Open University course DD203 *Power, Dissent, Equality: Understanding Contemporary Politics*. Details of this and other Open University courses can be obtained from the Student Registration and Enquiry Service, The Open University, PO Box 625, Milton Keynes, MK7 6YG, United Kingdom: tel. +44 (0)1908 653231, e-mail general-enquiries@open.ac.uk

Alternatively, you may visit the Open University website at www.open.ac.uk where you can learn more about the wide range of courses and packs offered at all levels by The Open University.

For availability of other course components visit the webshop at www.ouw.co.uk, or contact Open University Worldwide, Michael Young Building, Walton Hall, Milton Keynes MK7 6AA, United Kingdom for a brochure. tel. +44 (0)1908 858785; fax +44 (0)1908 858787; e-mail ouwenq@open.ac.uk

Living Political Ideas

Edited by
Geoff Andrews and Michael Saward

Edinburgh University Press

in association with

TheOpen
University

Edinburgh University Press Ltd
22 George Square, Edinburgh

First published 2005 by Edinburgh University Press Ltd; written and produced by
The Open University

© 2005 The Open University

Edited, designed and typeset by The Open University.

Printed and bound in the United Kingdom by the Alden Group, Oxford.

A CIP record for this book is available from the British Library.

ISBN 0 7486 1971 2 (hardback)

ISBN 0 7486 1972 0 (paperback)

1.1

Contents

Powers & structures

Centre & periphery

Participation & dissent

Equality & difference

Evidence & argument

The Open University course team

Geoff Andrews, *Staff Tutor in Government and Politics*

Brian Ashcroft, *Associate Lecturer Panel*

Pam Berry, *Compositor*

Karen Bridge, *Media Project Manager*

Vivienne Brown, *Professor of Intellectual History*

Julie Charlesworth, *Lecturer, Open University Business School*

Martin Chiverton, *Media Production Specialist*

Stephen Clift, *Editor*

Lene Connolly, *Print Buyer*

John Craig, *Associate Lecturer Panel*

Michael Dawson, *Course Manager*

Marilyn Denman, *Secretary*

Andrew Dobson, *Professor of Politics*

Lucy Flook, *Course Manager*

Fran Ford, *Course Secretary*

Liz Freeman, *Copublishing Advisor*

Robert Garson, *Reader in American Studies*

Pam Garthwaite, *Course Manager*

Carl Gibbard, *Graphic Designer*

Bram Gieben, *Staff Tutor in Government and Politics*

Janis Gilbert, *Graphic Artist*

Richard Golden, *Production and Presentation Administrator*

Montserrat Guibernau, *Reader in Politics*

Lisa Hale, *Compositor*

Celia Hart, *Picture Researcher*

Richard Heffernan, *Lecturer in Government and Politics*

Wendy Humphreys, *Staff Tutor in Government and Politics*

Jef Huysmans, *Lecturer in Government and Politics*

Bob Kelly, *Staff Tutor in Government and Politics*

Paul Lewis, *Reader in Central and European Politics*

Joanna Mack, *Media Production Specialist*

David Middleton, *Staff Tutor in Government and Politics*

Jeremy Mitchell, *Lecturer in Government and Politics*

Raia Prokhovnik, *Senior Lecturer in Government and Politics and Deputy Course Team Chair*

Michael Saward, *Professor in Politics and Course Team Chair*

David Shulman, *BBC Producer*

Lynne Slocombe, *Editor*

Mark J. Smith, *Senior Lecturer in Government and Politics*

Grahame Thompson, *Professor of Political Economy*

Consultant authors

Richard Freeman, *Senior Lecturer in Politics, University of Edinburgh*

Deborah Mabbett, *Lecturer in Politics, Brunel University*

Mads Qvortrup, *Professor of Sociology and Public Policy, The Robert Gordon University, Aberdeen*

Judith Squires, *Senior Lecturer in Politics, University of Bristol*

Nicholas Watson, *Professor of Disability Studies, University of Glasgow*

External assessor

Michael Moran, *Professor of Government, University of Manchester*

Preface

Tumultuous events such as '9-11' and the war and its aftermath in Iraq have reminded people how critical – and sometimes how deadly – the world of politics can be. Even the local, everyday politics of council services, schools and hospitals can affect people's lives powerfully. The Open University, with its unique tradition of interdisciplinary work and its mission to reach and enthuse a hugely diverse student audience, has set out to show why and how politics matters. It aims to shed light on the inner workings of power, decision making and protest, covering politics from parliament to the street, from ideas to institutions. *Living Political Ideas* is an accessible introduction to political ideas such as legitimacy, national self-determination, dissent and social justice. All too often political ideas are thought to be separate from the practical world of politics. This book shows how ideas live, both in the sense that all of us live with the consequences when they are put into practice, and that they change and adapt over time. Using historical and contemporary examples, the book represents a readable and critical introduction to political ideology and theory.

Series preface

This book is one of the five texts which make up the new *Power, Dissent, Equality: Understanding Contemporary Politics* series from The Open University. Each book in the series is designed for students and others who have not studied politics before, and can stand alone as a short introduction to key areas of debate within political science. However, if you wish to use the series as a whole, there are a number of references to chapters in other books in the series and these are easily identifiable because they are printed in bold type.

Each book offers a distinctive angle on the character and analysis of politics today. *What is Politics?* offers a critical overview, showing the often surprising faces and locations of political life. *Exploring Political Worlds* examines comparative politics, asking what we can learn by looking at one country or context in the light of another. *Politics and Power in the UK* questions how we might make sense of major developments and debates in UK politics, such as devolution and constitutional change. *Living Political Ideas* is an accessible introduction to key topics in political theory and ideology, such as legitimacy, national self-determination, dissent and social justice. *Making Policy, Shaping Lives* teases out and interrogates the many faces of public policy and policy making, drawing on case materials ranging from the single European currency to disability politics.

For all of the books, apart from *What is Politics?*, the chapters follow a common thematic structure. There are five organizing themes. *Powers and structures* explores the meaning and location of power in contemporary societies – what it is, and who has it. *Centre and periphery* looks at issues from the role of the state in our lives to the revival of nationalism in the post-Cold War world. *Participation and dissent* leads us to look, on the one hand, at voting and elections, and on the other hand at new and unconventional forms of political protest and dissent. *Equality and difference* examines how we are seen as 'equal to' and 'different from' each other and how this matters politically. The *evidence and argument* theme focuses attention on the ways in which the study of politics involves both explanation and recommendation.

Courses produced by The Open University are very much a team effort, and *Power, Dissent, Equality: Understanding Contemporary Politics* is no exception. Each member of the course team has made his or her mark on these books, and the work was done with goodwill and good humour. Some special thanks are owed. Raia Prokhovnik's tireless and dedicated contribution as Deputy and Acting Course Chair has been of huge benefit to the course. Mike Dawson has been a superbly calm, tactful and efficient Course Manager. Lucy Flook, Course Manager in the early days, played a significant role in getting the team up and running efficiently and ahead of schedule. Pam Garthwaite kept the momentum going in the period between Lucy's departure and Mike's arrival. The editorial skills of Stephen Clift and Lynne Slocombe and designs by Carl Gibbard have been key to the quality of the texts. Fran Ford has been a great support as course secretary, ably supported at different times by June Ayres and Marilyn Denman. John Craig and Brian Ashcroft have constituted a 'tutor panel' which has commented most helpfully on draft chapters. Robert Garson (Bobby) of Keele University was an influential and insightful member of the course team for two years. Professor Mick Moran of the University of Manchester has been the ideal external examiner – sharp and committed, he has been a tremendously positive influence on the content of these books.

Michael Saward, Course Team Chair

Introduction

Michael Saward and Geoff Andrews

More than once in recent decades we have heard about the 'end of ideology'. It was first discussed in the late 1950s, and emerged again in the 1990s. In the UK, for example, Tony Blair's New Labour government, first elected in 1997, stressed its pragmatic credentials, where it claimed it was driven not by ideology but by 'what works'. It stressed its role as the delivery of policy free of ideological constraints, arguing that this characteristic would distinguish it from previous governments of both left and right. Ideology in New Labour's eyes was regarded as an obstacle to practical politics.

Do examples like that of New Labour mean that ideas matter less in the politics of the UK and elsewhere today? Our response in this book is a resolute 'no'. There is no such thing as 'what works' on its own. Every policy and political argument, every party manifesto and candidate's speech, makes assumptions about people, the rights of citizens, the proper role of government, freedom and equality, order and change and so on. One might even say that ideas in politics are sometimes especially powerful if they remain unspoken, or their role denied or hidden. Unsurprisingly, New Labour's own non-ideological ideology has been the subject of much discussion amongst political theorists.

This book offers a brief and focused intervention into contemporary debates about the place of ideas in politics. Slim as it is, it is evidently not a guide to any and every political idea out there. Rather, our overall aim is both simple and challenging: to show that theories, ideology and ideas 'live'. They can be said to live in two senses – first, ordinary people live their consequences in particular historical settings and, second, they change and adapt with the rhythms of political life. Think, for example, of citizenship. It makes a huge difference in people's daily lives if their governments regard citizenship primarily in terms of duties rather than rights, or see its realization through the operation of a free market rather than through civic participation in public life. What it means to be a citizen has changed over time and has depended at various moments on the provision of civic, democratic or social rights. The modern idea of citizenship has been understood and articulated within the context of the nation-state. More recently, political theorists and students of politics have turned their attention to the impact of globalization and how this might affect the status of the citizen, and indeed the *idea* of citizenship.

Ideas are crucial to politics. For something to be 'do-able' politically, it must first be thinkable. For a political party or an interest group to be formed and to compete effectively with others, some idea of what it might represent, or fight to achieve, will be essential. It will unavoidably have to set out a vision of a better world and a strategy that is aimed to get us there. Even government departments, whose jobs are normally seen as 'mere' administration and which are staffed by 'non-political' civil servants, rely on ideas about, for example, what governments should be doing and whether the public they are dealing with should be understood as dependants, clients, consumers or citizens. How we view governmental and other institutions often seems like common sense to us. But the present shape of our political institutions only seems normal and natural because it is familiar, and often without thinking we accept the ideas on which their very existence depends. But ideas do live and change, adapt and re-form. In the UK less than one hundred years ago, for example, the idea that the state should be deeply involved in economic and social life would have been unthinkable.

The category 'political ideas' is a huge one and political ideas come in different forms. One specific distinction which forms a thread throughout this book is that between political theory and political ideology. *Political theory* is the term most often used by professional academics who teach and write about political ideas. Just what political theory is, these and others would dispute – some might even say a large part of the subject is exactly the debate about what it is, and where its boundaries lie. Political theory often includes the study of 'great works' from centuries past, going back to Plato's *The Republic*, Hobbes's *Leviathan*, Locke's *Two Treatises of Government*, Rousseau's *The Social Contract*, Mill's *On Liberty*, Marx and Engels' *The Communist Manifesto* and so on. Such a list would now include contemporary works as well, most notably John Rawls's *A Theory of Justice*. The ideas of many of these works are discussed in the following pages, though, crucially, within particular contexts and to inform particular debates. The works of the 'great thinkers' should not be seen as removed from contemporary political events or isolated from current debates. For example, in Chapter 3 Mill's work is discussed in the context of contemporary debates on liberty, while Rawls is applied in Chapter 4 to help us understand the meaning of social justice.

Political theory also normally encompasses the analysis of key *concepts* in politics, such as equality, freedom, justice, rights, democracy and citizenship. These are discussed in different contexts in the chapters that follow. It can help us to explain and understand, for example, the distribution of power between citizens and the state (the focus of Chapter 1), as well as the forging of political identities by national communities *across* nation-states (discussed in Chapter 2). Political theory can also be recommendatory or prescriptive – concerned with the 'ought' as well as the 'is'. This is what we mean by *normative* political theory especially. Indeed, Rawls's theory, for example, recommends that we see justice in a certain way, as making certain specific demands on states and citizens. We will see in Chapter 1 that *prudential* political theories are concerned with 'ought' questions in a slightly different way.

Political ideology, on the other hand, is seen here as a set of ideas which offers a particular interpretation of the world and its problems, accompanied by recommendations about what should be done to make the world a better place. For example, a (certain type of) Marxist would recommend revolutionary overthrow of the capitalist system and of the state which supports it, given the systematic exploitation of the working class under that system. Or a (certain type of) liberal would recommend getting the state 'off people's backs', so as to enhance individual freedom and choice. Ideologies, too, have their descriptive and prescriptive elements – their 'is' and their 'ought'. Does ideology overlap then with normative political theory?

Certainly it does. Ideology is often seen as embedded in politics, in the sense that it is attached to parties, political figures, manifestos and policies, while political theory is more often seen (for better or worse) as separate from or 'above' the immediate political cut and thrust – more reflective, more systematic, abstracted more from the immediate context. However true these claims may be, when we look at the differences between these categories we are dealing with matters of degree and not absolute differences.

This book is deliberately selective. We offer snapshots of living political ideas. Which ideas and which debates we discuss in the five chapters that follow are driven in part by the five themes which we wish to examine: powers and structures, centre and periphery, participation and dissent, equality and difference, and evidence and argument. Our choices are also driven by the relevance of these topics to contemporary politics. The ideas that form the focus of the book are: political legitimacy, self-determination and nationalism, dissent, and social justice. In addressing these ideas – as living political ideas – all the chapters make important links between concepts, political theory and ideology.

Chapter 1, written by Vivienne Brown, asks: where does the state get its legitimacy from? What can legitimize relations between the leaders and the led? It will take you through some of the classics of political theory, including the work of Hobbes, Locke, Rousseau, Hume and Bentham, in order to establish what is at stake in discussions of legitimacy. What are the 'invisible bonds of political society'?

Chapter 2, by Michael Saward, focuses on the question: is there a right to self-government? Who can define such a right? Does self-government necessarily mean secession? What about dissenting minorities and the impact on those from whom a group decides to secede? The focus is on nationalism and theories of self-determination. It will also reflect on images of the nation, contested meanings of nations and on the impact of nationalism as an ideology.

Chapter 3, by Geoff Andrews, discusses the significance of dissent for politics and argues that as a living idea it has served to 're-invent' politics at different times. This chapter gives a historical overview of the place of dissent in British politics since the 1700s and how it became identified with different thinkers as well as its impact on political change. The chapter analyses different modes of dissent and ends by taking up Michael Freeden's argument that ideology is the 'vehicle of dissent'.

Chapter 4, by David Middleton, discusses social justice primarily through the work of John Rawls and his key critics. At the core of this chapter is the link between social justice and equality. What do these concepts mean and how should they define the way society is organized? The impact of 'difference' on debates about equality and social justice is also a feature of this chapter.

Chapter 5, by Mark Smith, reflects on the ways in which political ideas are debated and studied as exemplified in the preceding chapters. On what *grounds* have arguments about foundations of authority, the rights to secede or dissent, or the goal of equality been put forward? What are the boundaries between ideology and political theory? Is there an ideal standpoint we can adopt to understand the role of political theories?

All five chapters argue that ideas are crucial to politics. This includes the meanings of political concepts and the analytical approaches of political theories, as well as the durability of political ideology. In order to understand the role they play we need to see them as living political ideas embedded in particular contexts and open to change and rejection, contest and adaptation. We believe that studying them in this way will enable a sharper and more focused appreciation of the breadth of politics itself.

Political legitimacy

Vivienne Brown

Contents

Powers & structures

1   THE INVISIBLE BONDS OF POLITICAL SOCIETY

May Day demonstrations against 'globalization' had become an annual feature of the international political landscape by the end of the last century. Some who participated at these demonstrations were anarchists who challenge the assumption that the authority of the state is necessary for societies to be well organized – and who, as one part of this, provocatively challenge key symbols of national culture and history (see Figure 1.1). Anarchists may disagree amongst themselves on the economic arrangements of society, with some supporting free markets and others supporting economic collectivism, but they share an opposition to the state as the ultimate source of political authority. Anarchists argue therefore that the state has no political legitimacy.

The question of the political legitimacy of the state has attracted the attention of political theorists, not because they are sympathetic to anarchism, but because there is a question as to how to reconcile citizens as individuals – as autonomous individuals – with the authority of the state. In considering this, theorists have also been responding to the big political issues of their own time which raised fundamental questions in new ways, but these fundamental questions continue to live on and so later theorists in their turn have tried to provide better answers for their own societies.

The legitimacy of the state is taken for granted by many people for most of the time, that is, most people support the state under which they live and accept their own obedience to the laws of that state. By this I don't mean that people support their own state and obey the laws out of fear of punishment, but rather that people recognize that living under the state implies that they support that state and obey its laws. Political legitimacy thus provides the 'invisible bonds' of political society, holding it together in spite of the diverse interests and identities of different individuals, groups and classes within society. It is only in moments of intense political upheaval, such as during a revolution, that this political legitimacy is thrown into doubt as citizens' political support and obedience is questioned or withdrawn.

The system of laws is backed up by the power of the state. This includes the police force and armed forces, administration of the law, and the penalties and punishments that are enforced in the case of non-compliance with the law. The invisible bonds of society

FIGURE 1.1   A question of political legitimacy: the statue of Winston Churchill after an anti-capitalist demonstration, May Day, 2000

are backed up by links that are as tough as steel. Political legitimacy thus connects with the entire system of 'powers and structures' that support the laws that citizens live under and help maintain the state's authority. Political authority is legitimate in a formal sense when the provisions of a country's constitution are adhered to, for example when laws are made and administered properly according to constitutional rules (see **Heffernan, 2005**). The question of political legitimacy that we are examining in this chapter is not concerned with formal legitimacy, but with the larger question of citizens' obedience to the laws.

Acceptance of political legitimacy doesn't imply that there is no room for questioning or challenging particular laws or aspects of political society. Political legitimacy is compatible with forms of political dissent which criticize and try to change particular laws and practices, as Chapter 3 explains, and this may include specific acts of civil disobedience which involve public breaches of the law. For example, the suffragettes at the beginning of the twentieth century in Britain engaged in acts of civil disobedience in order to bring attention to their campaign for votes for women. Many reform movements that we now regard as right and just also included acts of civil disobedience at the time; for example, the civil rights movement in the USA and the anti-apartheid movement in South Africa.

Different political theorists have put forward different explanations to account for political legitimacy. We shall examine some influential theories that attempt to explain political legitimacy, and in doing this we shall be looking at some 'classics' in political theory that have framed the ways in which these questions have been analysed.

Some of these classic works were written at a time when the society of the day was (or had recently been) undergoing political upheaval, and so these theories bear the hallmarks of the intense theoretical questioning that political uncertainty and violence prompted at the time. But even if these theories bear the marks of their own time, they also raise political issues of long-standing interest and relevance that later political theorists have worked with or challenged. In this way they form part of our intellectual and historical legacy; over the years these theories have filtered through into everyday discourse about politics and they live on in the language of current debates.

As an introduction to these debates I shall focus on three approaches to asking questions about political legitimacy.

- *Normative* approaches to the question of political legitimacy look for the reasons why citizens *ought* to support the state and obey its law, in the sense that the reasons for this relate to what it is morally right for autonomous individuals to do. This approach sees the question in terms of 'political obligation', so the challenge is to explain the 'obligation' or 'moral duty' that citizens have. The basic question that encapsulates the normative approach is: '*why ought* citizens to support the state and obey its law?'

- *Prudential* approaches don't look for moral reasons or the grounds of a political obligation to support the state and obey its law. Instead, they focus on the utility or self-interest of doing so. According to this approach, an explanation of political obedience can be found in reasons connected to people's self-interest. The basic question that encapsulates the prudential approach is: '*why do* citizens support the state and obey its law?'

- Theorists who employ *constructivist* approaches think that both normative and prudential approaches have misunderstood the issue in looking for reasons *why* citizens obey the state. According to a constructivist approach this misconstrues the nature of political processes: citizens may think that they are acting autonomously according to their reasons, but because they are 'inside' the political processes that mould them they can't see how their actions and responses are constructed by the requirements of those processes. Thus, the constructivist approach formulates the question of political legitimacy as a 'how' question: '*how are* citizens rendered supportive and obedient to the state under which they live?'

These three approaches to posing the question of political legitimacy can be seen at work in some of the major 'classics' of political theory. It would be an oversimplification to say that these classic writings only ever display just one of these three approaches; but different theorists have tended to adopt one way rather than another of framing the question, so, as an introduction to these theorists, it is helpful to cast our discussion in terms of these three approaches. In Sections 2 to 4 I shall take each of these basic approaches in turn as one way of framing the question about political legitimacy, and I shall illustrate each by selections from classic texts in political theory. In Section 5 I'll reconsider the theories and highlight some similarities and differences across them.

SUMMARY

- Political legitimacy is about the obedience of citizens to the state under which they live.

- This chapter examines a number of 'classic' texts on political legitimacy.

- Three approaches to political legitimacy are considered: normative, prudential and constructivist.

2 NORMATIVE THEORIES OF POLITICAL LEGITIMACY

Normative theories look for the grounds of citizens' support and obedience in a moral obligation to obey the state, and so the question for them is the nature and source of this moral obligation. One starting point is the individual's freedom and will. This approach is sometimes termed 'voluntarism' because it is rooted in the voluntary actions of autonomous individuals. The question of political legitimacy then concerns the reasons why individuals voluntarily accept limitations on their freedom by obeying the state's laws. One answer is to see this obedience as the result of a promise, agreement or contract to obey the law. This 'social contract' approach to obligation as the basis of political legitimacy has been immensely influential in Western political theory.

2.1 Hobbes's absolutism

One version of this argument is given by Thomas Hobbes (1588–1679) in *Leviathan* (1651). This was the period of the English Civil War. Two years before the publication of *Leviathan*, in 1649, King Charles I had been executed at Westminster. These were dangerous times. Hobbes was a royalist, although in his own life he took the oath of allegiance to the Commonwealth during the Interregnum period, after the death of Charles I, on the grounds that a strong state was needed for securing internal peace. The most important characteristic of the state for Hobbes was thus that it should be a strong state in providing security for its citizens.

As with all social contract theories, the starting point is a 'state of nature', a situation where people are thought of as living under natural law but without any politically organized society. The question that the theorist asks is: what would people in a state of nature, without a government or political organization, do? Although the state of nature is imaginary, it is a device we can use to think about what is important for politics, the state, and legitimacy. As you might imagine, the political conclusions theorists draw depend very much on the kind of life envisioned in this state of nature. Hobbes argued that all individuals (by which he understood males only) have a natural 'liberty' to do whatever they think is needed for their own preservation. This derives from Hobbes's view of liberty, sometimes termed 'negative' liberty (see Box 1.1), meaning liberty or freedom from the interference of others, or the liberty to do whatever is not actually forbidden by the law.

> ### BOX 1.1   **Negative liberty/freedom**
>
> One of the most influential descriptions of 'negative' liberty is in Isaiah Berlin's essay 'Two concepts of liberty', originally delivered as an inaugural lecture at the University of Oxford in 1958 (Berlin, 1969). Berlin's distinction between 'negative' and 'positive' liberty isn't entirely straightforward and has been given different interpretations, but the gist of it is that negative liberty is liberty from external obstruction, interference or constraint, whereas positive liberty, by contrast, concerns self-mastery or the capacity to act in an appropriately fulfilling way. For example, you are negatively free in reading this chapter if no one is preventing you from doing so (it isn't censored, for example), but you are positively free in reading it if you are exercising self-mastery by exercising a capacity for rational argument and controlling your lower-order desires to, say, go partying instead. The negative concept has been criticized for leaving out social and economic factors that curtail people's capacity to act; to take the classic example, anyone has the negative freedom to dine at the Ritz – no one is actually stopping you – but few people can afford to do it.

In spite of the existence of natural law, without a political authority to keep the peace, this natural liberty has few constraints and so Hobbes's state of nature is a fearful place:

> Hereby it is manifest, that during the time men live without a common Power to keep them all in awe, they are in that condition which is called Warre; and such a warre, as is of every man, against every man. For Warre, consisteth not in Battell onely, or the act of fighting; but ... where every man is Enemy to every man ... wherein men live without other security, than what their own strength, and their own invention shall furnish them withall. In such condition, there is no place for Industry; because the fruit thereof is uncertain: and consequently no Culture of the Earth; no Navigation, nor use of the commodities that may be imported by Sea; no commodious Building; no Instruments of moving, and removing such things as require much force; no Knowledge of the face of the Earth; no account of Time; no Arts; no Letters; no Society; and which is worst of all, continuall feare, and danger of violent death; And the life of man, solitary, poore, nasty, brutish, and short.
>
> (Hobbes, 1991, Part I, Chapter 13, pp.88–9; first published 1651)

Hobbes's argument is that in the absence of a common power to make and enforce laws, a state of nature must be a war of all against all; not because everyone is always fighting, nor that everyone wants to fight, but that if there is uncertainty for everyone over their own safety and whether they will have enough material goods to survive, then the threat of having to fight for survival is always present. In such a situation of fear and insecurity, the refinements and advantages of society and human effort, foresight and the use of intelligence would be impossible, Hobbes argued.

One image of the Hobbesian state of nature is that it is peopled by individuals who are egoistic and aggressive in furthering their own self-interest. According to this reading of *Leviathan*, the fearfulness of the state of nature is a result of the egoism and selfishness of human nature. But another reading suggests that the same outcome of a war of all against all would also follow if a kinder interpretation were made of human nature. According to this reading, the crucial point about the state of nature is people's basic insecurity concerning their own safety and others' intentions towards them. On this reading, Hobbes's interpretation of human nature is softer, but the outcome of a war of all against all would be more or less the same.

Whatever the final judgement on human nature, Hobbes's solution to this 'solitary, poor, nasty, brutish, and short' way of living is for mankind to leave the state of nature by voluntarily placing restrictions on their liberty and promising amongst themselves to obey central laws. This way they can eliminate insecurity and live peacefully. The question is: how can this be done? The first law of nature is to seek peace, so, having regard only to their own safety and security, all individuals make a contract between themselves

FIGURE 1.2   Detail from the engraved title page of the first edition of *Leviathan*

to confer their natural liberties upon some man or assembly of men, which is the sovereign. All these individual powers would thus be invested in the sovereign, so that individuals are thereafter taken to will (or to want) whatever it is that the sovereign wills. The moral grounds for citizens' obligation thus lies in the promise or contract to obey the sovereign. It is also the case, however, that the all-powerful sovereign demands obedience from its subjects. There is a strong prudential element in political obedience to the sovereign, since the consequences of not obeying could be serious indeed.

The result is that subjects can have no grounds for complaint against the sovereign, which has more or less absolute authority over them, except for example in cases of self-defence (scholars are in debate as to just how absolute the sovereign really is). This sovereign is Leviathan, the all-powerful figure which was illustrated on the original title page of the book and which is reproduced in (or on the cover of) some modern editions of the book (see Figure 1.2).

If you look closely you'll see that Leviathan's body is composed of many tiny individuals. The illustration thus pictures how the sovereign's power is derived from all the individual powers that the subjects have voluntarily given up and transferred to the sovereign. In this way the sovereign becomes the sole source of power and so there are no other rival sources of power in society, either political or religious, that can challenge the authority of the sovereign. Hobbes's account of political legitimacy is thus thoroughly secular, allowing no independent political power for organized religion, something which made enemies for him at the time. Hobbes's absolutist conclusions also shocked many of his contemporaries, and later reworkings of the social contract approach to political obligation challenged Hobbes's absolutism.

2.2 Locke's constitutionalism

The classic account of what has come to be seen as a liberal 'social contract' theory was put forward by John Locke (1632–1704) in the *Two Treatises of Government*, first published in 1689 (dated 1690). Although this was published less than 40 years after *Leviathan*, the political climate had shifted considerably. Locke probably wrote it during 1679–83 amidst fears that Charles II was becoming absolutist and when Locke himself was possibly connected with political activities against the crown, fleeing to Holland for his life where he lived in exile from 1683 to 1689. The *Two Treatises* was thus probably originally inspired as a justification of resistance against what was feared to be a potentially absolutist state, whereas Hobbes's *Leviathan* was aimed more at safeguarding a strong secular power following the devastating experience of civil war. Locke was concerned with spelling out restrictions on state power by specifying the limits of political obedience, whereas Hobbes was trying to safeguard political security by setting limits on challenges to state power. Each was putting forward an innovative theory, but each was influenced by the political events of the time.

The *Two Treatises* has come to be regarded as a classic statement of the
principles of political liberalism. (The term 'liberal' was not used in English
politics until the early part of the nineteenth century; the term in use in
Locke's time and during the eighteenth century was 'Whig'.) Like Hobbes,
Locke also used the device of the state of nature but his portrayal of it was
less fearsome than Hobbes's. One reason for this difference lies in the
emphasis given to the religious and moral underpinnings of Locke's state of
nature, and another lies in the greater material provision for human needs
because God's care is taken to ensure adequate subsistence for all. Most
famously, the laws of nature allow for individual private property rights:

> God, who hath given the World to Men in common, hath also given them reason
> to make use of it to the best advantage of Life, and convenience. The Earth, and all
> that is therein, is given to Men for the Support and Comfort of their being. And
> though all the Fruits it naturally produces, and Beasts it feeds, belong to Mankind in
> common, as they are produced by the spontaneous hand of Nature; and no body
> has originally a private Dominion, exclusive of the rest of Mankind, in any of them,
> as they are thus in their natural state: yet being given for the use of Men, there
> must of necessity be a means *to appropriate* them some way or other before they
> can be of any use, or at all beneficial to any particular Man.
>
> (Locke, 1988, *Second Treatise*, paragraph 26, pp.286–7; first published 1690)

Locke's argument here is that God gave the world to mankind in common for
them to use and enjoy, but what an individual works on belongs to that
individual and no one else has any right to it. This is the basis of Locke's
argument that individual property is based on a person's labour in gathering
or hunting the means of subsistence in the state of nature; by extension, this
argument is then applied to the cultivation of land and other forms of
productive labour. This argument for individual property rights provides a
means of securing an orderly existence in the state of nature, since the laws of
nature include the right to property, that is, more generally, the right to 'life,
liberty and estate' (the word 'property' for Locke is thought to have had this
broader meaning). This enables Locke to provide a more harmonious picture
of the state of nature than Hobbes had done. Crucially, however, Locke's
argument also goes on to establish that these natural rights to life, liberty and
estate, which pre-exist political society, are not to be violated by the state after
political society has been set up.

Although Locke's state of nature is not threatening in the way that Hobbes's is,
it lacks the advantages of political society, such as impartial judges and a
system of law for adjudicating disputes between individuals. (In the state of
nature individuals are judges in their own case.) One of the advantages of
setting up political society is to have 'known and indifferent judges' to ensure
an impartial resolution of disputes according to law. Individuals therefore
agree, on the basis of the exercise of their reason, to set up political society;
and part of the objective of doing this is to protect their natural rights to life,
liberty and estate.

> Men being, as has been said, by Nature, all free, equal and independent, no one can be put out of this Estate, and subjected to the Political Power of another, without his own *Consent*. The only way whereby any one divests himself of his Natural Liberty, and *puts on the bonds of Civil Society* is by agreeing with other Men to joyn and unite into a Community, for their comfortable, safe, and peaceable living one amongst another, in a secure Enjoyment of their Properties, and a greater Security against any that are not of it. ...
>
> And thus every Man, by consenting with others to make one Body Politick under one Government, puts himself under an Obligation to every one of that Society, to submit to the determination of the *majority*, and to be concluded by it; or else this *original Compact*, whereby he with others incorporates into *one Society*, would signifie nothing, and be no Compact, if he be left free, and under no other ties, than he was in before in the State of Nature.
>
> (Locke, 1988, *Second Treatise*, paragraphs 95, 97, pp.330–2; first published 1690)

Free individuals consent to be governed by being party to a compact according to which they exchange some natural rights, such as their right to judge in their own cases, in return for the state's protection of their remaining natural rights, such as their rights to life, liberty and estate. Individuals voluntarily 'put on the bonds of civil society'; their obedience to the state is based on their promise to obey in return for the state's preservation of their rights to life, liberty and estate. The similarity with Hobbes's account is that citizens (or rather subjects in Hobbes's case) voluntarily surrender something of their natural freedom in return for the protection of the state. A difference lies in the kind of agreement that is made, since, for Locke, the powers of the state are limited by the terms of the compact.

This implies that the state is legitimate only if it honours the terms of the compact in protecting individuals' rights. This has formed the basis for what has come to be the classic 'liberal' case for constitutional government based on the 'social contract'. For example, in the case of taxation, a hotly debated issue over the years, if individuals have a natural right to their property, then according to the Lockean argument taxation is just (or reasonable) only if it is undertaken with their consent. In liberal states, this normally means that taxation policy requires the broad consent of the citizens. That consent provides the moral foundation of taxes and the obligation on all to pay them. If the state acts beyond its powers or if it does not fully respect the natural rights of its citizens, then the state is breaking the social contract and so forfeits its right to citizens' support and obedience. The social contract between citizens and state thus defines the limits of political obligation. The lasting implication of this argument is that the state has a duty to protect and promote the natural rights of its citizens, and that citizens' political obligation is conditional on the state's fulfilling its side of the contract. This is the classic liberal argument for limited constitutional government. It provides a moral foundation for political obligation but it also justifies civil disobedience and other forms of dissent which are directed at changing specific areas of society or the law (as you will see in Chapter 3). It also provides moral grounds for withdrawal of consent and resistance against a state that fails in its duty.

Deriving from Lockean arguments, liberal social contract theory regards 'free' political relations as contractual in character; the parties to the contract freely enter into it, and are then bound by its terms. This model of liberal contractual relations has also led to a massive growth of various 'rights discourses' in modern Western society. Rights imply that there is some other party against whom the right is held and which has a specific duty to the right-holder (for example, if I have a right to an education, then someone else, usually the state, must provide it to me). Rights talk presupposes 'reciprocal' bonds between the holders of the rights and the holders of the duties, whether between individual citizens or between citizens and the state. The significance of rights discourses can now be seen across the entire political, social and economic spectrum: political rights such as the right to vote and the right to freedom of speech; civil rights movements for the same political and legal rights for all citizens irrespective of gender or ethnicity; women's rights to control their bodies; children's rights; gay and lesbian rights not to be discriminated against on the basis of sexual orientation; economic rights such as the right to own and sell property, the right to engage in contracts with others, and workers' rights to a job or to a fair wage, or the right to strike; animal rights; ecological rights, and so on. The United Nations *Universal Declaration of Human Rights* (1948) and the Human Rights Act 1998 in the UK refer to a wide range of rights covering political, social and legal rights.

The classic liberal theory of political legitimacy has thus provided the theoretical resources for the growth of rights movements that took place during the twentieth century and which is still continuing. This discourse of rights now provides the main vocabulary for political argument concerning justice, inequality, oppression and dissent, as you will discover in later chapters in this book, so that opposing arguments in political debate are often both expressed in terms of rights, raising the important question of how such rights can be justified. Some political theorists have questioned whether this proliferation of 'rights talk' has devalued the currency of 'rights' as a normative concept.

WHERE'S THE BIT ABOUT THE RIGHT TO CHEAP DIESEL?

The invisible bonds of political society thus comprise a network of reciprocal rights and duties that define the relations that hold society together. This network is not static but is constantly being contested and redefined as new rights demands enter the political arena, both from the left and the right, and from new political movements. The reciprocal nature of rights and duties between citizens and the state can also be understood in different ways with respect to the extent of legitimate state power. At one end of the spectrum there is a minimalist or libertarian 'night-watchman' version, where the state's duties are restricted to maintaining basic public services, defence, law and

SMALLTIME TRANSPORT

order (see the discussion of Nozick's theory of justice, for example, in Chapter 4). At the other end is the vision of an interventionist social-democratic welfare state based on extensive state provision of economic security and the availability of education and health services. In practice, however, governments themselves are frequently the violators of individual rights.

2.3 Rousseau and the general will

Jean-Jacques Rousseau (1712–1778), author of *The Social Contract* (1762, published in French), lived during the *ancien régime* of aristocratic privilege in France, and like many other eighteenth-century philosophers was something of a polymath. He was a musician, novelist and botanist, for example, as well as a political philosopher. Rousseau was a stern critic of modern society, however, and challenged contemporary views about the progressive nature of civilization and the benefits of the development of the arts and sciences. For inspiration Rousseau frequently looked to natural man uncorrupted by what he saw as the vanities, inequalities and injustice of modern society. He also admired the small civic societies of ancient Greece, with their more direct forms of participatory government (for free male citizens, that is). In this he may have been influenced by the experience of his early life in the small mountainous state of Geneva, although he spent much of his later life in France.

In *The Social Contract*, however, Rousseau argued that natural man's freedom was an inferior kind of freedom and that a more developed freedom was possible only in political society. Rousseau thus challenged the argument of earlier social contract theorists that some freedom has to be sacrificed for political obedience in order to have the protection of the state and its laws. Far from accepting any incompatibility between individual freedom and political security, Rousseau argued that individual freedom would be *enhanced* by means of a contract to set up political society.

Rousseau's understanding of the relation between individual freedom and political obedience was thus entirely different from that of either Hobbes or Locke, and this was in part because he had a different notion of freedom as 'self-mastery'. Rousseau's notion of freedom is a version of the 'positive' concept of freedom, in contrast with Hobbes's 'negative' freedom (see Box 1.1). The notion of 'freedom' is thus a *contested concept*: such concepts take on different meanings in different theories or in being put to different uses as part of the repertoire of living ideas in political debates.

For Rousseau, freedom takes on a moral quality in a well-ordered society: 'moral freedom, which alone makes man truly master of himself; for the impulsion of mere appetite is slavery, and obedience to the law one has prescribed to oneself is freedom' (Rousseau, 1997, I.8, p.54; first published 1762). For Rousseau the thought of renouncing any moral freedom was anathema, and so he rejected the idea that mankind could give up some freedom for political obedience. His solution was to argue that if each person fully participates in the making of the law, then, in obeying that law, the person is obeying only himself and so is fully free. It is in the formation of the 'general will' that the resolution of freedom and obedience, man and citizen, was to be found. The aim of the social contract was therefore as follows:

> 'To find a form of association that will defend and protect the person and goods of each associate with the full common force, and by means of which each, uniting with all, nevertheless obey only himself and remain as free as before.' This is the fundamental problem to which the social contract provides the solution. ...

> If, then, one sets aside everything that is not of the essence of the social compact, one finds that it can be reduced to the following terms: *Each of us puts his person and his full power in common under the supreme direction of the general will; and in a body we receive each member as an indivisible part of the whole.*

> At once, in the place of the private person of each contracting party, this act of association produces a moral and collective body made up of as many members as the assembly has voices, and which receives by this same act its unity, its common *self*, its life and its will.

> (Rousseau, 1997, I.6, pp.49–50; first published 1762)

Thus freedom is obedience to the law if that law is what you have prescribed for yourself. This is because the general will is the will of any citizen when putting the general interest first. The general will thus provides a means of collective rule by popular sovereignty according to which each person seeks the general good, rather than his or her private or particular good. The idea is that in obeying the general will each person is obeying himself. In participating in the 'general will' men achieve a 'moral freedom' in political society that is impossible in the state of nature where they are dictated by appetite rather than reason.

Rousseau's argument was a rejection of social contract theories which argued that some freedom must be foregone by living in political society. In his version of social contract theory, man's (moral) freedom could be realized only in political society with the collective rule of popular sovereignty. Rousseau was a critic of the domination and inegalitarianism of the hierarchical society of his own time; the general will was proposed as a way of having both a more just and democratic political society, and a higher moral aspiration for citizens as human beings. The general will was meant to overcome the distance and tensions between the individual and political society that the other social contract theorists had also grappled with. On the other hand, in spite of Rousseau's emphasis on freedom and equality, the identification of a person's freedom with what the law prescribes, and the resulting equation of 'freedom' and 'obedience', introduces the threat of political coercion and even totalitarianism. If no one may challenge the general will, on the basis that this is what they would seek if they were thinking of the general good, this opens up the possibility of citizens being forced to play a key part in their own subjection, all in the name of their higher freedom. Indeed, in a famous passage of *The Social Contract*, Rousseau argued that people can be 'forced to be free' – an argument that many liberal theorists have found shocking.

The influence of this argument has been immense, although interpretations of it have varied enormously. The philosophy of Immanuel Kant was influenced by the notion of personal freedom as self-rule or 'autonomy'; and Rousseau's emphasis on popular sovereignty, freedom and equality has been thought to have been influential for the French Revolution which took place a few decades after he wrote. Rousseau's argument provides a collectivist or communitarian explanation of political obligation, within the social contract tradition: citizens' political obedience is to a law that they have given themselves collectively. Far from reducing their own freedom, obedience to the general will is meant to represent the full achievement of their moral freedom. In this way Rousseau attempted to reconcile the requirements of political obligation with the requirements of individual moral freedom.

2.4 Social contract theories

As we have seen, there are different types of social contract theory. The core idea is that political obligation is based on the consent of free individuals, rather than on tradition or force. The power of the idea of consent as 'contract', however, may reflect a society that has become increasingly commercial, so that the invisible bonds of political society are now to some degree represented in terms of the contractual bonds between economic agents exchanging their goods. It may be that the influence of social contract arguments has arisen partly from the growing importance of commercial contractual relations as well as the increased political significance of freedom and individual rights.

Social contract theories have, however, been subject to a number of criticisms. One criticism concerns voluntary consent. If this consent was given way back in the mists of time, how does that govern our political life *now*? It seems inconceivable that each generation should be bound by the original consent given by their ancestors so long ago. Perhaps the original contract and associated consent are just hypothetical, in that each generation would give its consent if asked to renew the social contract. But on what grounds would people give their consent in the present day? This raises afresh the question of the grounds for political obligation: might it be based on individual grounds of obligation, on individual benefits, or on the general good? Another response might be to interpret the social contract not as an original or actual contract but as an 'implicit' contract such that modern generations give their 'tacit' consent to be governed just by living under the state and enjoying its protection. But a problem with this argument is that most citizens have little choice in the matter as they are unable to simply uproot themselves to live in another place. Furthermore, it is even harder to find a place to live without any state at all, and so it is not practically possible for people who wish to withhold consent to do so by choosing not to live under any state. Where could an anarchist go and live? On the other hand, this argument concerning tacit consent is sometimes used in connection with people coming to live in a country, in that their choosing to settle in that country implies a tacit consent to obey the laws of that state.

Another sort of criticism is directed to the idea of a state of nature. It is meant to identify key features of human society, but it has been criticized as a 'fiction' that transposes certain features of social and political life into a supposed pre-political state in order to provide a spurious 'natural' justification for them. Locke's 'natural' right to property is a case in point. Similarly, the notion of individuals as living outside a political community, yet endowed with just those individual rights and duties that characterize modern Western society, is also criticized on the grounds that it presents a Westernized view of human society as if it were an eternal truth. Furthermore, it is argued, social contract theories promote an abstract concept of the 'individual' without the cultural identity, gender, economic positioning, ethnic or national loyalties, and so on, that go to make up the 'real' individuals living in political societies and which affect individual life chances and political roles.

In the abstract, all are equal (have equal rights) in social contract theories. The criticism that this view masks real inequalities has been taken up by Marxist writers and is discussed in Section 4.1 below. It has also been taken up by some feminist theorists who have argued that the abstract individual of theories of political obligation is actually gendered, as a male, and that accounts of natural 'man' in the state of nature carry patriarchal (or limited and male-dominated) notions about gender. According to this view, it is not sufficient just to include women along with men in these accounts, or to say that 'man' is a generic term for a human being. They argue that social contract accounts are based on a patriarchal conception of power, and that the social contract is built upon a 'sexual contract' in which women are subordinated, despite the fact that the social contract theories don't reveal this part of the story (Pateman, 1988). Modern relations of contract, it is argued, are not the epitome of liberal freedom but provide the means by which unequal political powers are sanctioned and protected.

In spite of these criticisms, the impact of social contract theorizing on Western political thought has been enormous. We can also see important links between some classics of social contract theory and modern democratic ideas. Locke refers to the way in which, as a result of the social compact, each individual 'puts himself under an Obligation to every one of that Society, to submit to the determination of the *majority*' (Locke, 1988, paragraph 97; first published 1690). This raises a question of what or who constitutes the 'majority'. In Locke's time, this majority was of propertied males. Rousseau introduces the notion of the general will as representing the general good. In the modern world the grounds of political legitimacy have also come to be seen as deriving in some way from 'the people', and modern Western liberal theories of political legitimacy (whether or not based on social contract theory) are now based on democratic ideas of universal suffrage that imply some kind of popular sovereignty or mass legitimation (e.g. Beetham, 1991).

SUMMARY

- Normative theories of political legitimacy look for the basis of citizens' moral obligation to support the state and obey its laws.

- Social contract theories attempt to explain the moral basis of political obligation in terms of citizens' voluntary consent, individually or collectively.

- Influential examples of social contract theory are those of Hobbes, Locke and Rousseau, although the political implications of these theories are very different.

- Social contract theories derive reasons for political obligation by using the notion of a 'state of nature' as a way of exploring the political relations of modern society.

- Hobbes's version of social contract theory provides arguments for the absolute power of the secular sovereign, Leviathan.

- Locke's version of social contract theory provides the basis for a liberal account of limited constitutional government and it provides the theoretical resources for the modern development of 'rights' discourses.

- Rousseau's version of social contract theory provides a collectivist account of popular sovereignty according to which, in obeying the general will, citizens are obeying a law they have given themselves.

- 'Freedom' is a contested concept; different theorists attach different meanings to it.

3 PRUDENTIAL THEORIES OF POLITICAL LEGITIMACY

In this section we'll look at two examples of a prudential approach to political legitimacy. Prudential theorists reject the idea that there is a political obligation or a moral duty to obey, and so they also reject the entire social contract tradition. They argue that citizens obey the law because it is in their interests to live in political society with the protection of a state. Social contract theorists also accept that it is in the citizens' interest to live in political society and obey the laws; in this sense there is a prudential element in social contract arguments too. The difference is that the social contract theorists think we need more than that – in their view, there also has to be a moral argument to explain political obedience as political obligation. Prudential theorists argue that the social contract theorists are wrong in this respect. They think that the prudential argument on its own is sufficient to explain political obedience without recourse to political obligation.

3.1 Hume's theory of utility

David Hume (1711–1776) was a Scottish philosopher and historian, a contemporary and acquaintance of Rousseau, who was writing in a more settled and prosperous period than either Hobbes or Locke. Hume was critical of social contract theorizing. One reason for this was that he thought it was futile to try to derive features of mankind's social and political arrangements by abstracting from the actual course of historical development. In common with some other eighteenth-century philosophers, Hume emphasized that the institutions of the state evolved in response to the developing needs of human society, and so he did not use rationalistic (or religious) arguments to explain features of political society.

Hume took this argument even further and turned the notion of 'natural' into the opposite of what the social contract theorists argued. Hume argued that 'property' and 'justice' could be said to be 'natural', not in the sense that they derived from a state of nature, but because of their obvious utility or 'interest' to human society so that they emerged 'naturally' as a result of the development of human conventions. In this way, Hume likened political notions such as 'property' and 'justice' to the development of languages, which were introduced 'naturally' as part of a gradual process based on human conventions without any promise or contract.

Hume also argued that the idea that mankind could set up political society by making a contract is unconvincing because the notion of a 'promise' or a 'contract' is itself a product of society; in this sense the social contract theorists were assuming what they were setting out to demonstrate. The 'state of nature' was thus for Hume a 'philosophical fiction' that obscured rather than helped to explain political relations (Hume, 1978, III.ii.2; first published 1739–40).

For Hume, political support and obedience (or 'political allegiance' as he sometimes called it) is based on the practical necessity of having laws to control antisocial behaviour and on the existence of the state's power in enforcing those laws. Hume didn't try to ground political obligation or the requirements of justice on normative or rationalistic considerations. His argument for political obedience was prudential in stemming from what he saw as the requirements of social life, since government is necessary to enforce laws and maintain justice in developed societies. Hume saw no need to seek further justification for this political obedience or to ground political obedience in obligation.

Like Locke, however, Hume would not defend absolutism. As the purpose of the state, he argues, is to provide security, then the state ceases to be legitimate and obedience to it ceases if the state no longer provides this or itself becomes a source of insecurity and oppression. This was how he explained it:

> ... interest ... [is] at once the original motive to its [the government's] institution, and the source of our obedience to it. This interest I find to consist in the security and protection, which we enjoy in political society, and which we can never attain, when perfectly free and independent. As interest, therefore, is the immediate sanction of government the one can have no longer being than the other; and whenever the civil magistrate carries his oppression so far as to render his authority perfectly intolerable, we are no longer bound to submit to it. The cause ceases; the effect must cease also.
>
> (Hume, 1978, III.ii.9, pp.550–1; first published 1739–40)

Here Hume is arguing that interest (that is, utility or public interest) provides the reason why people obey the state; if the state becomes tyrannical or otherwise no longer serves the public interest, then there is no longer any reason for people to obey it. Thus, Hume's prudential argument for the legitimacy of state power also specifies the limits of that legitimacy. Hume's argument for limited government and his concern with freedom is thus in alignment with Locke's liberal conclusions, but the argument supporting it is entirely different.

Hume's arguments were criticized because of their attack on traditional arguments about the basis of morality and justice (and religion), but his arguments against social contract theory were taken up enthusiastically by Jeremy Bentham.

3.2 Bentham's greatest happiness principle

Jeremy Bentham (1748–1832) was a philosopher and reformer who wrote on law, government and economics. Bentham agreed with Hume that utility provides the fundamental reason why people obey the law and that utility also determines the acceptable limits of political authority. In *A Fragment on Government* (1776) Bentham subjects the social contract tradition to withering scorn and claims that it is a fiction that introduces muddle and confusion. One moment, he argues, its exponents accept that there never was such a contract in a historical sense, yet the next moment they argue that 'in nature and reason' the social contract is implied by political society. Bentham thought that this kind of argument was utter nonsense (Bentham, 1988, pp.37–8; first published 1776), although a social contract theorist might reply that this criticism misses the point, in that the state of nature argument provides insights into modern political relations.

Bentham, along with Hume, argued that the idea that political obedience is based on a promise or contract made no sense, since the reason for keeping promises is exactly the same as the reason for obeying the law: that is, utility. Trying to explain political obligation by the keeping of promises was evidence of confused thinking according to Bentham. This is how he put it:

> This then, and no other, being the *reason* why men should be made to keep their promises, viz. that it is for the advantage of society that they should, is a reason that may as well be given at once, why, *Kings*, on the one hand, in governing, should in general keep within established Laws, and (to speak universally) abstain from all such measures as tend to the unhappiness of their subjects: and, on the other hand, why *subjects* should obey Kings as long as they so conduct themselves, and no longer; why they should obey in short *so long as the probable mischiefs of obedience are less than the probable mischiefs of resistance*: why, in a word, taking the whole body together, it is their *duty* to obey, just so long as it is their *interest*, and no longer. This being the case, what need of saying of the one, that *he* PROMISED so to *govern*; of the other, that they PROMISED so to *obey*, when the fact is otherwise?

> (Bentham, 1988, p.56; first published 1776)

According to Bentham, promises – just like political obedience – are based only on interest or utility. His 'should' here is thus based on a utilitarian argument.

Bentham's notion of interest or utility is that of the greatest happiness of the greatest number: his greatest happiness principle. This appears in the passage above where he refers to the 'probable mischiefs' of one or other course of action. Bentham argued that the best course of action would be the one with the greatest amount of happiness and the least amount of pain. He went even further than this and also argued that his greatest happiness principle provided a 'standard of right and wrong' (Bentham, 1988, p.58; first published 1776). According to Bentham, the moral question *why ought citizens to support and obey the state?* is meaningless because it is based on the false idea that there are moral reasons for behaviour separate from prudential reasons. He argued that what is taken to be morally right in any society simply is what produces the most happiness. In this his argument is similar to Hume's, that what is taken to be morally right is that which is conducive to human utility.

Bentham was also critical of the notion of 'natural' rights. The notion of 'right' is generally held to imply a correlative 'obligation' or 'duty' on another party. For example, the right to an education implies that there is some other party, say the government, which has the duty to provide the education. It follows from this that rights always imply duties on others which are enforceable by law or by some other means, or else they are meaningless. Bentham argues that there are no such things as 'natural' rights because in the state of nature there is no means of enforcing the correlative duties. In Bentham's words, natural rights are 'simple nonsense', and 'natural and imprescriptible rights' are 'nonsense upon stilts' (Schofield *et al.*, 2002, p.330). Here Bentham was criticizing the *Declaration of the Rights of Man and the Citizen* (1789, 1791) in France at the time of the Revolution. He argued that legal rights are backed up and made effective by being enforceable by law, but that 'natural' rights are not backed up by anything and so amount to nothing. Furthermore, legal rights are not fixed for all time (imprescriptible) but should be changed, on utilitarian grounds, when circumstances change. Talk of natural rights is thus not about existing rights but is rather about the legal rights that people wish to see in place. A modern example of this might be given by the UN *Universal Declaration of Human Rights* (1948), since the point of the UN *Declaration* is to make a statement about the need to establish legal rights for citizens.

SUMMARY

- Prudential theories argue that political legitimacy derives from the utility, interest or happiness of those governed.

- Influential prudential theories of political legitimacy are those of Hume and Bentham.

- Both Hume and Bentham argued that prudential reasons were sufficient to explain political legitimacy, and that supposedly independent moral reasons were in fact prudential reasons.

- Bentham's principle of utility is the principle of the greatest happiness of the greatest number.

4 CONSTRUCTIVIST THEORIES OF POLITICAL LEGITIMACY

In this section we turn to approaches which ask *how* citizens are rendered obedient to the state. These theories argue that legitimacy is produced or constructed as part of the practices of society, and that it is these practices that need to be understood. They argue that seeking for reasons to explain why people do things, whether these are moral reasons or prudential reasons, is to search in the wrong place.

4.1 Marxist theories of state power

Karl Marx (1818–1883) was writing at a time of economic, technological and cultural transformation of the major European countries. He developed his ideas in Germany, France and England, involving himself in proletarian struggles and also studying and writing in the famous Reading Room of the British Museum in Bloomsbury, London. The distinctive features of Marx's theory are the importance of class struggle as the engine of change and the significance attached to the economic aspects of society in helping to explain political, social, cultural and legal forms. According to Marx's 'materialist conception of history', changes in society are influenced by changes in the 'mode of production', that is, changes in the material means by which society reproduces itself. For example, as the mode of production changed from the feudal system to the capitalist system of factory production, other changes in society's politics and law also followed; in the British case, for example, the political power of the House of Lords necessarily diminished as land became less important economically compared to the rising urban commercial classes.

Marx's theory of state power thus challenges social contract theory by posing a class-based – rather than abstract individualist – interpretation of political legitimacy. It argues that political relations are not the result of agreement between free individuals, or between citizens and the state, but are influenced by the economic structure of society. Fundamentally, the basis of political power is economic power, so that state power largely reflects and supports the interests of the dominant economic class. Each stage in history is characterized by its distinctive form of economic and class structure, and it is this that largely drives state power. In capitalist society, the dominant economic class is the capitalist class, which owns the means of production, and so it is their interests that ultimately influence the direction of the capitalist state.

Marx's model of the relation between economic interests and state power may be illustrated in terms of a spatial metaphor of an economic base and a

FIGURE 1.3 Engraving of the Reading Room of the British Museum, London, 1897

political, legal (also cultural) superstructure. The idea here is that the economic base is a fundamental influence on the ideas and norms which people use to make sense of politics and society, and which also serve to legitimize the needs of the ruling class. In *The German Ideology*, an early (unpublished) work written with Friedrich Engels in Germany during 1845–46, this is explained as follows:

> The ideas of the ruling class are in every epoch the ruling ideas, i.e. the class which is the ruling *material* force of society, is at the same time its ruling *intellectual* force. The class which has the means of material production at its disposal, has control at the same time over the means of mental production, so that thereby, generally speaking, the ideas of those who lack the means of mental production are subject to it. The ruling ideas are nothing more than the ideal expression of the dominant material relationships, the dominant material relationships grasped as ideas; hence of the relationships which make the one class the ruling one, therefore, the ideas of its dominance.

> (Marx and Engels, 1970, p.64; written 1845–46, first published 1932)

So the dominant ideas at a given time about, for example, art, literature, education and culture generally, are ideas which in a deeper sense reflect the interests of the dominant class – in our 'epoch', the capitalist class. As the ruling ideas are the ideas of the ruling class, those who are not members of the ruling class will be acculturized into accepting ideas that go against their own class interests. In capitalist society, this implies that workers (that is, those who must sell their labour power in order to support themselves) will face major and often subtle pressures to adopt ideas, including political ideas, that are beneficial to class interests that are not their own. Workers are thus led to acquiesce in their own exploitation by accepting the ideas of the ruling class.

The analysis of Marx and Engels has been criticized for overemphasizing the importance of economic factors and class membership, and neglecting the importance of other social, cultural and political factors. A continuing element in their thinking, however, was that the political power of capitalism was held in place partly by the ruling 'ideology' that reflected the interests of the capitalist class although purporting to express universal values which all classes in society could subscribe to. Workers' acceptance of this ideology was thus a form of 'false consciousness' that goes against their true class interests. The political ideas of the society were a part of this ideology, which therefore included the notions of 'political legitimacy', 'political obligation' and 'right of contract'. According to Marx and Engels, these notions are 'ideological' in that they purport to signify universal categories based on the notion of an equality of all citizens, as citizens, while masking the real facts of economic inequality and exploitation. It is in this sense that Marx and Engels referred to 'ideology' as a society-wide set of dominant ideas which in fact reflect the interests of the dominant class above all others. (As we saw in the Introduction, this is one sense of ideology among others; the following chapters will illustrate other senses of this key term.)

According to Marx and Engels' theory of ideology, the formal equality of all citizens, as posited in social contract theories, is an illusion since what's really important for people is their membership of an economic class. Thus, the notion of 'political obligation' obscures the fact that the laws necessarily work against the interests of the majority class, and that talk of rights gives a false impression of equality before the law. To ask what are the moral grounds of political legitimacy and political obedience is, therefore, they argue, to ask the wrong question, a question which is not objective because it already reflects biases of dominant ideology.

Marx and Engels' answer to the question of how political power endures in any society would not be expressed in terms of 'bourgeois' categories such as 'political legitimacy' or 'political obligation'. Instead their answer would refer to the actual practices of capitalist society in which the system of laws furthers the interests of capital and the pursuit of profit. Their basic answer to the question of resistance was of course posed in terms of the need for workers to overthrow the state in a workers' revolution; far from endorsing the 'invisible bonds' holding together class society, in *The Communist Manifesto* (1848) Marx and Engels called upon workers to throw off their chains (Marx and Engels, 1952, p.94; first published 1848).

4.2 Foucault and discourses of power

Another version of a constructivist theory of political legitimacy derives from the work of Michel Foucault (1926–1984), a French philosopher and historian of ideas at the Collège de France in Paris. Foucault was earlier influenced by Marx but he came to reject the economic emphasis of Marx's theories and the Marxist idea of ideology as false consciousness. Foucault was explicitly concerned with the '*how* of power' (Foucault, 1980, p.92).

Foucault contrasts his own account of power with the juridical or legal accounts of political power. Foucault argues that a social contract approach such as Hobbes's focuses on state power, the will of the sovereign and the rights of subjects/citizens. In opposition to this, Foucault argues that the relations of power extend beyond the limits of the state. He sees power as operating through networks of control and self-control that extend beyond the state and operate in every aspect of life, including the family and kinship, the body and sexuality, and discourses of knowledge and technology. Foucault's researches thus include investigations into the history of psychiatry, medicine, the penal system and sexuality, histories that Foucault termed 'genealogies' and which were aimed at challenging conventional notions of the proper focus of historical and political enquiry.

For Foucault, a 'discourse' is a set of ideas, statements and practices that construct a particular knowledge and so make that kind of knowledge and associated practices possible. For example, the discourse of 'crime' not only constructs our notions of the 'criminal' and 'criminality', but also forms part of the legal and penal practices, such as systems of surveillance and control in penal regimes, that put into effect the implications of those notions. Discourses thus have real effects in terms of the practices and techniques of the exercise of power. This also includes the techniques of the 'self' for governing oneself. Foucault argued against a dominant Western notion of an essence of oneself by showing how the self too is 'constructed' and 'governed' by the discourses and practices of society. Foucault also examined how different notions of 'madness' are produced in the practices of control and incarceration of psychiatric patients. One result of this approach is that individuals are not portrayed as more or less autonomous, separate persons or subjects, as they are in the state of nature theories of writers such as Hobbes and Locke. Rather, individuals are *formed* by those practices. A key result for Foucault is thus that individuals as subjects (both political subjects and subjects of experience) are constituted by the relations of power. This is how Foucault put it:

... rather than ask ourselves how the sovereign appears to us in his lofty isolation, we should try to discover how it is that subjects are gradually, progressively, really and materially constituted through a multiplicity of organisms, forces, energies, materials, desires, thoughts, etc. We should try to grasp subjection in its material instance as a constitution of subjects. This would be the exact opposite of Hobbes' project in *Leviathan*, and of that, I believe, of all jurists for whom the problem is the distillation of a single will – or rather, the constitution of a unitary, singular body animated by the spirit of sovereignty – from the particular wills of a multiplicity of individuals. ... rather than worry about the problem of the central spirit [of the sovereign, Leviathan], I believe that we must attempt to study the myriad of bodies which are constituted as peripheral *subjects* as a result of the effects of power.

(Foucault, 1980, pp.97–8)

Foucault argues that the focus for understanding how discourses of political power work is to analyse how individuals are constituted as subjects. Returning to the illustration of the figure of Leviathan, referred to in Section 2 above, we could say that, whereas Hobbes's interest was in the constitution of Leviathan, the sovereign figure, as composed of the individual bodies, Foucault's interest was in the constitution of all the individual bodies which are formed to make up the figure of Leviathan.

Foucault's conception of political power is an active or productive one in that it forms or moulds subjects in a particular way. Power is thus seen as a 'productive network' that works its way through people and society. But Foucault's analysis of power extends even further than this in that discourses themselves are also caught up in relations of power. Foucault argues that truth and power are not separate from each other. Discourses function within regimes of power and yet discourses are also the means by which truth is established: 'truth isn't outside power, or lacking in power ... truth is a thing of this world' (Foucault, 1980, p.131).

Foucault's work thus becomes a general analysis of power and the constructedness of our ideas of ourselves. His work has been criticized for an overemphasis on 'discourse' and the extent to which subjects are moulded or constituted by social and political practices. But the distinctiveness of his approach lies in the argument that political legitimacy is achieved as part of a much wider set of practices, and is produced as part of the generalized 'how' of power. Foucault argues that to struggle against power as if it could be overcome, diminished or localized, is to misconstrue the pervasive necessity of power, since relations of power are a ubiquitous feature of any society. Political resistance can thus only be aimed at changing the relations of power by changing the discourses and practices of power; but in doing this it is futile to think that it is also possible to stand outside or be released from all discourses or relations of power.

Returning to the notion of political legitimacy as the 'invisible bonds' of political society, we could say that for Foucault these bonds are not something that individuals rationally or consciously take upon themselves for moral or prudential reasons, or can deliberately cast off when they become oppressive; but rather that these bonds are the threads by means of which political and social relations are already woven into the fabric of society. (On Foucault see also **Lewis, 2005**.)

SUMMARY

- Constructivist theories of political legitimacy examine how citizens are rendered obedient.
- Influential constructivist theories of political legitimacy are those of Marx and Foucault.
- According to Marx's theory of ideology, political legitimacy has to be understood in terms of the economic interests and ideology of class society.
- According to Foucault's analysis of power, political power has to be understood as part of the broader '*how*' of power.
- 'Ideology' is a contested concept.

5 ANALYSING POLITICAL LEGITIMACY

This chapter has discussed some influential writings on political legitimacy in terms of three broad approaches: normative, prudential and constructivist. But such a classification is itself just one possible organizing device. It brings to light certain similarities and contrasts between the different theories, but other organizing principles could have been chosen and these might have emphasized different conceptual or analytical relations between the different approaches.

We have seen that social contract approaches seek justification of individuals' obedience to the state in an agreement or contract to do so, thus attempting to reconcile what is taken to be the autonomy of individual wills with the reality of political support and obedience. The political implications of such an approach turn out to be varied, comprising the absolutism of Hobbes, the constitutionalism of Locke and the ambiguities of the popular sovereignty of Rousseau. We also saw that this involves different notions of 'freedom', a contested concept. For Hobbes, freedom is negative freedom or the freedom to act in the absence of restraint (or in the silence of the law); and Bentham agreed with this. For Rousseau, on the other hand, freedom involves living according to the law one has made for oneself, a form of self-mastery by means of which people live according to the rules they have set for themselves. This is a version of positive liberty and it appeals to an idea that people need certain conditions to achieve fulfilment (rational or 'true' fulfilment), and the mere absence of restraint is not enough. In some respects this is akin to Marx's approach to human nature as requiring certain material and social conditions for its fulfilment. Foucault, on the other hand, argued against the idea of an essential 'self' and was interested in the ways in which notions of the self were produced in different discursive contexts.

Locke and Hume both argued against absolute state power yet they did so from different positions. Locke argued from the state of nature to compact and consent, whereas Hume dismissed state of nature arguments and social contract theories. Locke emphasized the importance of human reason in knowing the laws of nature and natural rights, and also in agreeing on the social compact. For Locke the origins of political society thus lie in the rational powers of mankind to work out what would be the right thing to do. Hume, on the other hand, was against rationalist explanations of human behaviour and social/political practices. He argued that reason was the slave of the passions and so he emphasized the importance of the desires and wants that motivate people to action. According to Hume, explaining human behaviour thus required understanding people's motivations – their emotions and sympathetic feelings – as well as the importance of convention in the historical evolution of human development.

Religion also features differently in the various theories. Locke's state of nature is often taken to be the epitome of individualism, but for Locke it was governed by the law of nature which is God's law. This God is the Christian God, or rather a Protestant God; and the importance of this religious starting point implies that the overall meaning of Locke's works registers his deeply held Christian beliefs. Marx, on the other hand, applied a materialist understanding to religious ideas; like all ideas in society, he argued, they can be understood largely in terms of the economic relations of the time. Thus he would argue that the idea of God is a part of the ideological superstructure of society, and is 'constructed' as part of this broader ideology which provides a justification of the economic relations of society. According to this view, Locke's religious ideas would need to be considered in terms of the working out of the Protestant Reformation in the context of economic changes that were taking place, rather than solely in terms of the particular spiritual biography of an individual person named John Locke.

Both Marx and Foucault focus on the 'how' of power. Foucault was influenced by Marx, but he was also critical of what he termed the 'totalizing' tendency of theories such as Marx's, which purport to explain everything in terms of overarching laws or tendencies. Foucault was more interested in the particularity of different practices, although he also provided some larger theorizing in his account of the role of discourses and relations of power. Both Marx and Foucault argue that the inculcation of ideas in society is crucially important, although Marx's account of ideology as false consciousness suggests that workers might escape the delusions of ideology after the revolution in a non-exploitative society, whereas Foucault argues that thought and analysis can never escape the governing power of discourses.

Many of these theorists also analysed the power of words and 'concepts'. Hobbes analysed the power of words in naming moral ideas and he was aware of the effects of rhetoric (for good and ill) in communication and writing. Locke too was troubled by what he saw as the ambiguity of words and he noted the potential power (and even pleasure) of rhetorical uses of language which may deceive the unwary. A problem for Hobbes was that part of the need for a sovereign was to ensure a common and correct naming of political and legal terms, an approach that is far from Foucault's call to contest discursive meanings as a way of contesting particular forms of power. The importance of this question of meaning and language also has modern resonances in current political debates about government 'spin'. Seen in a wider perspective, the issue of political 'spin' is not solely about justifying specific policies to the present government's benefit, but also about controlling the terms of political debate itself. The Bush and Blair administrations, for example, in the debate leading up to the invasion of Iraq of 2003, framed debate about 'the war on terror' in terms of 'security' and 'weapons of mass destruction'. As many important political terms are 'contested concepts' (we have seen two examples in this chapter: 'freedom' and 'ideology'), it matters in political debates how terms are used and what particular meanings are given to them. Political ideas live on; and how they live matters to political outcomes.

The question of the control or the play of language in political debates returns us to the issue of *who* is participating in such debates: who are the addressees of these arguments about support and obedience to the state? It was noted earlier that Western political debates now tend to presuppose that political legitimacy is a question of mass legitimation or popular sovereignty in some sense, although issues about democratic government also raise some controversial questions (**Lewis, 2005**). This also raises the question of who is included in this notion of 'the people'. At the time of writing for the classic political theorists whom we have studied in this chapter, the addressees were (largely) propertied males. Since then the property qualification has been disbanded and women have also been given the vote in democratic countries. The modern Western approach to political legitimacy links it with opportunities for democratic participation, so that democracy is now seen as a necessary condition for political legitimacy. This reminds us that the tradition of debate about political legitimacy that I have outlined in this chapter has been very much a Western European debate and that the notion of 'the people' is particular to that debate.

This raises a further (and final) question, this time about the spatial or geographical composition of 'the people'. In theories of political legitimacy a stereotype of a domestic state with its 'own' domestic population can easily emerge. Yet the actual histories of states are much more complicated than that. The modern nation-state as we understand it now is a relatively recent product historically, and the actual histories of modern nation-states have been marked with violent territorial wars, colonial rule or complicated migrations (including forced migrations) of populations over time. If political legitimacy is linked to popular sovereignty in the modern world, this leads us into questions of state building and national self-determination. This is the subject of the following chapter.

REFERENCES

Beetham, D. (1991) *The Legitimation of Power*, London, Macmillan.

Bentham, J. (1988; first published 1776) *A Fragment on Government* (ed. Harrison, R.), Cambridge, Cambridge University Press.

Berlin, I. (1969) 'Two concepts of liberty' in *Four Essays on Liberty*, Oxford, Oxford University Press.

Foucault, M. (1980) *Power/Knowledge: Selected Interviews and other Writings, 1972–1977* (ed. Gordon, C.), Brighton, Harvester.

Heffernan, R. (2005) 'Governing at the centre: the politics of the parliamentary state' in Heffernan, R. and Thompson, G. (eds) *Politics and Power in the UK*, Edinburgh, Edinburgh University Press/The Open University.

Hobbes, T. (1991; first published 1651) *Leviathan* (ed. Tuck, R.), Cambridge, Cambridge University Press.

Hume, D. (1978; first published 1739–40) *A Treatise of Human Nature* (ed. Selby-Bigge, L.A.; 2nd edn revised by Nidditch, P.H.), Oxford, Clarendon Press.

Lewis, P. (2005) 'Politics, powers and structures' in Lewis, P. (ed.) *Exploring Political Worlds*, Edinburgh, Edinburgh University Press/The Open University.

Locke, J. (1988; first published 1690) *Two Treatises of Government* (ed. Laslett, P.), Cambridge, Cambridge University Press.

Marx, K. and Engels, F. (1952; first published 1848) *The Communist Manifesto*, Moscow, Progress Publishers.

Marx, K. and Engels, F. (1970; written 1845–46, first published 1932) *The German Ideology*, London, Lawrence and Wishart.

Miller, D. (ed.) (1991) *Liberty*, Oxford, Oxford University Press.

Pateman, C. (1988) *The Sexual Contract*, Cambridge, Polity Press.

Rousseau, J.-J. (1997; *The Social Contract* first published 1762) *The Social Contract and Other Later Political Writings* (ed. Gourevitch, V.), Cambridge, Cambridge University Press.

Schofield, P., Pease-Watkin, C. and Blamires, C. (eds) (2002) *Rights, Representation, and Reform: Nonsense upon Stilts and Other Writings on the French Revolution*, Oxford, Clarendon Press.

FURTHER READING

Good overall introductions to political philosophy are given in:

Miller, D. (2003) *Political Philosophy: A Very Short Introduction*, Oxford, Oxford University Press.

Wolff, J. (1996) *An Introduction to Political Philosophy*, Oxford, Oxford University Press.

The Open University has an introductory text/course in political philosophy:

Warburton, N., Pike, J. and Matravers, D. (eds) (2000) *Reading Political Philosophy: Machiavelli to Mill*, London, Routledge/The Open University.

Good brief introductions to the theories of individual political philosophers are available in the Oxford paperback 'Past Masters' series and the Oxford 'Very Short Introduction' series (some of which are identical).

An accessible introduction to theoretical debates about political obligation is given in Horton, J. (1992) *Political Obligation*, London, Macmillan, although this is concerned only with what I have termed 'normative' theories of political legitimacy.

Them and us: national self-determination as a living political idea

Michael Saward

chapter

2

Centre & periphery

Contents

1 INTRODUCTION

We saw in Chapter 1 that political legitimacy involved the legitimation of power in a certain place, over people who are in a certain territory. Vivienne Brown reminded us that political theorists – classic writers such as Hobbes and Rousseau but contemporary ones too – have often assumed a neat fit between *this* government and *that* territory and its population, as if the fit between the two were somehow natural or timeless. Reality is always messier than that, of course. Countries, or nation-states, are in part constructed entities or communities – political units that are consciously demarcated and separated from others. As Guibernau comments, 'In seeking to *engender* a sense of belonging among its citizens the nation-state demands their loyalty and fosters their national identity' (**Guibernau, 2005, Section 3**, emphasis added).

Political theorists have only paid systematic attention to the constructed, engendered aspect of nationhood, and to the ideology of nationalism, in recent years. That is not surprising. For one thing, nations and nationalist movements are all unique in some way. Political theorists find nationalism difficult to generalize about, as opposed to a concept such as 'legitimacy' or 'freedom'. Further, most professional political theorists work in the rich northern countries, where national borders had been stable until the implosion of the Soviet Union in the late 1980s. The creation of new states in the ex-Soviet Union, civil wars over nationalist claims in ex-Yugoslavia, and events such as the splitting of Czechoslovakia between the Czech Republic and Slovakia, raised pressing questions of principle and revived interest in political units, borders and nationalism in countries from Italy to the UK to Spain. This renewed interest was also prompted by the revival of sub-nationalist movements. In the UK, for example, such movements played their role in the pressures that led to the establishment of the National Assembly for Wales and the Scottish Parliament. A number of political theorists responded to the challenging questions raised by these developments. In this chapter we shall take a critical look at some of the answers put forward, in terms of:

FIGURE 2.1 The end of the Soviet Union: Mikhail Gorbachev at a press conference, Moscow, July 1991

- belonging, loyalty, community and statehood

- the relationship between individual self-determination and collective self-determination

- the range of possible meanings of the idea of the 'nation'
- nationalism as a political ideology
- the debate on the 'right' to national self-determination: when is secession justified?

Forging, moulding, defending and stabilizing a nation-state – and having that nation-state recognized as legitimate by other, surrounding states – is a key way in which relations of *centre and periphery* are defined in modern politics. The existence of nation-states leads us to think of political centres and peripheries in certain ways, such as:

1 capital cities of countries as centres, the rest of the country as periphery

2 struggle over a city or other place as the centre for two or more communities, nation-states or would-be nation-states (e.g. Jerusalem in Israel and Palestine)

3 powerful countries as central, weaker countries as peripheral, in the international system

4 'Brussels' as centre, and the national capitals as periphery, in the European Union

5 English county councils as centres, and district and parish councils as peripheral, at the regional and local levels of the UK state.

What is central, and what is peripheral, depends on one's own perspective, of course, Brussels and London may seem peripheral to those absorbed in parish pump politics in a Derbyshire village – in that respect, centre and periphery are matters of perception as well as matters of power. Notice also that the list does not include what we could call functional or non-territorial centres and peripheries – those that are about power and practices rather than power and places, central activities rather than central institutions. That *is* an important part of any general discussion of political centre and periphery – as discussions of multi-level and network governance show (**Thompson, 2005; Charlesworth and Humphreys, 2005**). In this chapter I will focus on 'centre and periphery' through the specific filter of nationalism and national self-determination, not least because these ideas and practices have influenced crucially how we *locate, interpret* and *experience* political centres and peripheries in the contemporary world.

2 POLITICAL BELONGING: LOYALTY, COMMUNITY AND STATEHOOD

Which people, which group, do you belong to? How do we know who is Them, and who is Us? Where do your political loyalties lie? In a way these are simple questions. There are many contexts in our daily lives when we could answer them well enough. We speak common languages with people around us (and often with the same accent). Many of us live in neighbourhoods and recognize 'neighbours' as a distinctive group to which we belong. If we pray regularly in a mosque or church then we might identify ourselves with others as part of a 'community' there; if we drink regularly in the local pub or café we might feel the same. There can be many, overlapping communities, large and small, and we can belong to a range of them.

What about your primary political loyalty? Many people will happily see themselves and others as fellow British or French or Brazilians or South Africans, whatever other factors may separate them from some of their compatriots. This sense of belonging will generally transfer to accepting the French, Brazilian, etc., government as legitimate, however much one wants to see the policies or the composition of the current government change.

It is easy to say 'many people' will be able to identify, and feel comfortable with, their larger political loyalties or belongings (and it's an old trick of political theorists to invoke the 'many people would ...' defence for what they are arguing). Equally, many will not. People can be 'caught' without or between primary political attachments. On the one hand, many societies today are multicultural or multinational, their citizens having diverse, multiple and shifting loyalties. On the other hand, massive movements of people on a global scale have been evident in recent years, for example the movement of Afghanis and Iraqis to Europe and elsewhere in the 1990s and early 2000s in the face of war, oppression and poverty. Such massive movements of people make the experience of indeterminate loyalties and belongings – indeed, statelessness – a common experience. Further, many minority communities within nation-states commonly feel ambivalent about their compulsory primary loyalties, for example indigenous peoples in the USA, Canada, Australia and New Zealand.

> **BOX 2.1**   **Community**
>
> 'Community' is one of the most notoriously ambiguous terms in the vocabulary of politics. It can be and is used to refer to *any* collectivity or group of people, whether or not that group is large or small, aware of its 'groupness' or not, territorially contiguous, inclusive or exclusive, loosely or tightly structured, hierarchical or egalitarian, atomistic or organic, and so on. Politicians are well aware of the word's ambiguity and its feel-good character (how can 'community' be a bad thing?), deploying the term to suit their purposes. Social scientists are wary of using the term without due caution, as they are more often aware of the pitfalls that come with its ambiguity and contestability.

Many residents of places such as Macedonia, Kosovo, the Palestinian territories, Cyprus, so-called 'Padania' in northern Italy, Catalonia, the western Sahara, Abkhazia, Aceh, Scotland and Quebec live with constant questioning about what should be their primary political loyalty – *their* nation, or *their* country. Some will feel that an alien political identity is being imposed on them by a state they regard as illegitimate: the Israeli state in the Palestinian territories, the Moroccan state in the western Sahara, and the Georgian state in Abkhazia. Their literal neighbours may defend with equal vehemence their loyalty to those same states. Although at one level each case is unique, in many such places there is anguished and bloody conflict over legitimacy, loyalty and belonging. Strong sentiments can be fuelled by nationalist agitation and propaganda. Political struggles over land and identity can take the form of 'border disputes' at one extreme to 'ethnic cleansing' and 'civil war' at the other. The impact these conflicts have on the lives of many thousands of individuals and families are well documented (**Huysmans, 2005**). Nationalism and national self-determination are living political ideas that people do indeed live (and die) for.

The main reason that such conflicts are so important to leaders and followers caught up in them is that to achieve and sustain *statehood* for one's nation is the ultimate expression of political independence, as it has been since the rise of the modern nation-state around the time of the French Revolution. At that time, the nation-state began, for a complex variety of reasons, to see off its great historical rivals – city-states and empires for example. Beginning in Europe and spreading through colonial conquest and domination, the nation-state has become the basic political unit across the globe (**Gieben and Lewis, 2005**). Although the fact and the value of its primacy is much debated today, especially by strong advocates of 'globalization', it still provides the fundamental frame through which we understand the government of people and territory. There are local government units within countries and supranational governing institutions 'above' them (such as the European Commission and the European Parliament in the EU), but the nation-state is the basic, bedrock unit. There have been different theories about what can make political power legitimate. But when utilitarians, contract theorists, Marxists and others argue about political legitimacy they are almost always arguing about the rightful government of *nation-states*.

Because statehood is a prized possession, it is hardly surprising that fundamental political questions about 'them' and 'us' can invite strident answers: most Kosovan Albanians for instance are utterly adamant that they are not Serbs and should not be governed as part of Serbia. The Kosovan periphery in Serbia rebels against the centre, or what it sees as oppression of its own distinct identity by that centre. No case is that straightforward, of course. Up to the 1990s, Kosovans had not sought independence from Serbia, but rather civil rights. The wars in ex-Yugoslavia provided a context for the emergence of nationalism; other demands transformed into demands for national self-determination. In terms of general principles the case of Kosovo does raise the tricky question: where two or more resolute communities claim the same piece of territory as theirs, where each wants to be governed by people from (as they see it) their own group, who can decide what is right? Are there any broadly acceptable criteria to guide us when we ask who has a right to national self-determination in different cases or disputes?

I want to show how political theory has responded to fundamental questions thrown up by nationalism, the assertion of the right to self-determination, and the closely related rise in secessionist movements. As we shall see, there is no consensus. But theoretical debate has given us some refined and intriguing responses.

SUMMARY

- The nation-state remains the main political loyalty in the contemporary world.

- National loyalties are placed in question by increasingly multicultural and multinational societies, and massive global movements of 'stateless' people.

- Struggles for statehood are the basis of many serious conflicts around the world.

- We need to ask if there are political theory criteria to guide us in nationalist disputes.

3 SELF-DETERMINATION: INDIVIDUAL AND COLLECTIVE

The idea of a right to 'collective self-determination' is a difficult one – how can a group, as opposed to an individual, have a 'right'? To argue that a nation has a right to self-determination is, some might argue, to overlook what rights *are*, and who can claim them.

'Self-determination' has a positive ring about it – how could anyone oppose it? The idea of self-determination has strong resonances in political theory, dating back as far as Hobbes, at least in England. As we saw in Chapter 1, as European societies over the centuries became gradually more individualistic, so the idea of individual judgement and freedom gradually became more prominent. In the works of the great European political theorists of the seventeenth and eighteenth centuries, the idea of individuals consenting to – choosing, voluntarily – government restrictions on their freedom was crucial. Often political theorists talk of 'autonomy' as a principle, underlining the importance of separate, rational, thinking and choosing individuals as the core of political life. The idea of self-determination gets much of its resonance and attractiveness, I suggest, because it taps into this deep vein of thinking about individual rights, autonomy and freedom which runs through the Western body politic up to today.

However, *that* tradition is about individual self-determination. Even if it is a principle we could all sign up to, transferring it uncritically to a group or collective context creates problems. Can a *group* be said to have a 'will', or to be 'rational', in a way analogous to an individual? Can a group make decisions, for example about how to live or who to live with, with the same kind of conviction and clarity that an individual (sometimes) can? The problem is that in a large group there is often no unanimous view on any issue. How many members of a potential group would need to live together in a political community to make that community so legitimate that it could be imposed on dissenters? For example, if there is a 51 per cent vote for an independent Quebec in the coming years, is that enough to justify its imposition on the large minority in the province who opposed secession from Canada? If it was 70 per cent would that make a difference? How large or active or vocal does a dissident minority, who want a different community, have to be to challenge that legitimacy effectively? I will pick up some issues of majorities and minorities below; my immediate point is that the very idea of collective self-determination is problematic. Its proponents cannot draw easy support from the idea's linguistic link to the notion of *individual* self-determination. Perhaps the links between the two are more rhetorical than substantial.

Collective self-determination could mean various things, but most importantly today it means national self-determination: the idea that each 'nation' should be self-governing, i.e. it should have its own state. So, for example, Palestinians see themselves as a nation, and seek their own independent state so that they can be self-governing, and not be subject to governance by Israel (or any other state). Many Quebecois – mostly its non-immigrant francophones – regard their primary political loyalty as being to the Quebec nation, and they would like to live in a Quebec that is an independent country alongside Canada, rather than being a province within Canada's federal system.

It is worth noting that this fairly simple picture smooths over some important exceptions and complications. Collective self-determination *need not* mean outright statehood. It could mean instead some form of autonomy or self-government *within* another state. Many Quebecois are federalists, rather than nationalists; for various reasons, they prefer Quebec to remain within Canada, even if they favour considerable autonomous powers for the government of the province and special recognition of its francophone culture. Recently, Kurdish parties and leaders have broadly accepted that the predominantly Kurdish regions within Iraq, which might potentially be part of an independent state of Kurdistan, should instead be semi-autonomous regions within the federal, post-Saddam Iraq (see **Guibernau, 2005**, on definitions of federalism). However, these are exceptions to the rule that national self-determination is normally an aspiration to statehood.

The idea of national self-determination first came to prominence as part of the plans of US president Woodrow Wilson to rebuild Europe after the First World War. His famous Fourteen Points at the Armistice conference in 1918 set in motion a process of national self-determination across the war-torn continent. The Great War had destroyed the Austro-Hungarian empire, Germany, and the Russian and Turkish empires. A new way had to be found to organize government in the region. Wilson saw himself as involved in a process of constructing nations, and indeed many new states were created from the ex-empires. Some, such as Poland, were states based more-or-less on a group with a recognizable and felt common culture. Others, such as Yugoslavia and Czechoslovakia, were multi-nation-states, which dissolved into the constituent nation-states more recently (between 1992 and 2003, Yugoslavia broke into Slovenia, Croatia, Bosnia-Herzegovina, and Serbia and Montenegro; in 1992, Czechoslovakia divided into the Czech Republic and Slovakia in the so-called 'velvet revolution').

After the Second World War, a new wave of national self-determination accompanied the process of decolonization. Across Asia and Africa, through the 1950s and 1960s, several new independent states were formed out of the former British, French, Belgian, Dutch and Portuguese empires. This wave usually kept intact the political units that together made up empires; though there were major exceptions, such as the break-up of India into the two states of India and Pakistan (and later into three states, with east Pakistan becoming Bangladesh in 1971).

The meaning and application of the idea of national self-determination has evolved during the course of the twentieth century. Most recently, as we have noted, after the end of the Cold War, there was a strong revival of interest in national self-determination among political theorists and international legal theorists. Today, with many 'nations without states' asserting their right to self-determination, what can political theory tell us about identifying nations and specifying principles (and practices) of national self-determination?

SUMMARY

- National self-determination is one type of collective self-determination.

- The idea of collective self-determination gets much of its force from the analogy with deep-rooted ideas of individual self-determination or freedom; but shifting too easily from the individual to the collective can be problematic.

- A demand for national self-determination may not be a demand for outright statehood.

- The idea of national self-determination gained special prominence after the First World War.

- Interest from political theorists has been revived by the pressing nationalist demands in eastern Europe and elsewhere after the end of the Cold War.

4 WHAT IS A 'NATION'?

Clearly, the existence of nation-states defines a certain 'us-ness' and 'them-ness', which in turn plays a key role in creating a centre and its various peripheries, territorially at least. Guibernau (1996, p.47) has defined the nation as: 'a human group conscious of forming a community, sharing a common culture, attached to a clearly demarcated territory, having a common past and a common project for the future and claiming the right to rule itself'. So awareness, territory, history and culture, language and religion all matter. However, it is rare in the real world to find a case of a nation with a clear-cut and homogenous character in terms of this list of possibilities. Each nation is unique in the (alleged) makeup of its special character and worth. One crucial question is whether – and to what extent – a group must be *aware* of its alleged distinctiveness from other groups, in order to be classed as a nation. One could argue that a nation can *objectively* be defined as a group of people which possesses a shared and distinct, historically persistent cultural identity, and which makes up a majority within a given territorial area. If that is the case, then one could argue that even if such a 'nation' is not pushing for a right to self-determination (in any form), it nevertheless is a nation.

There are other would-be objective approaches to what might signify nation-ness, including statehood, ethnicity and naturalness.

- *Statehood.* This view holds that if a group has its 'own' state then it constitutes a nation. The common term 'nation-state' taps into this sense of nation. But this approach seems a little too neat, and begs many questions. For a start, it would mean that there can be no non-state nations, freezing into place the existing configuration of states that makes up the political map of the world. Defining nation-ness in terms of statehood, although common, rather rigs the game – why should all non-state 'nations' have their aspirations dismissed purely by definition?

- *Ethnicity.* Some interpret the principle of national self-determination as meaning that each 'ethnic' group forms a nation, and that each nation should be presumed to have a right to political self-determination. But who is to locate – and worse, to police – where the boundaries of one ethnicity stop and those of another begin?

- *Naturalness.* Mountains and rivers, for example, are sometimes thought to provide 'natural' borders. But, just as much as they divide and separate peoples, mountains and rivers and other features of the natural landscape can bring people together and create common interests and a common sense of community. There is no single or correct way to 'read' the social meaning of natural landscapes.

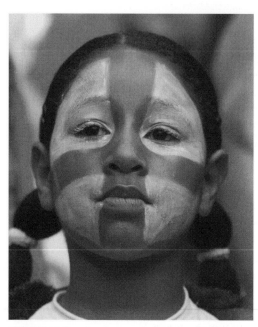

FIGURE 2.2 An expression of the English nation: a young football fan watches England v. Iceland

We can see that the problem with so-called objective approaches to defining a nation is finding sound criteria by which one might judge which groups form nations and which do not. How can we weigh different histories, traditions, religions, languages? Any attempt at objective demarcation of national communities is sure to remain contested, not least from among the groups who are thus classified.

This is why most theorists and observers adopt a *subjective* approach to defining nation-ness. From a subjective point of view, history, religion and language, for example, still count, but *awareness and acceptance* of a claim that X is a nation among the people of the supposed national group – a real consciousness that this is a group and I am part of it – is the crucial ingredient. This raises an important further question: does the awareness constitute the group, or the other way around? Certainly, a sense of nation and national belonging can be induced and engendered, 'created' if you like. Films, paintings, speeches and activities can invoke national heroes and national myths, which in turn can induce a sense of commonality and belonging. It normally serves the interests of those doing the inducing to say that they are merely reflecting what is already there, mirroring people's pre-existing and deep-rooted feelings of attachment. All of this is routine and familiar, on one level. All governments regulate, to some degree, citizen education, language, culture, sport, travel and so on, and by so doing they establish and reinforce some 'national' attributes and discourage others. But extreme, simplistic and coercive peddling of dubious 'national' myths for cynical power purposes is common enough also. Hitler's Nazism and Mussolini's Fascism were primary twentieth-century examples, but there are many others. As we shall see further below, nationalism has a dark side. It involves inevitable shoehorning of a people under a simplified set of cultural or other characteristics. The degree of this shoehorning and the way it is carried out are important.

From a subjective point of view, to quote Margaret Moore,

> the term 'nation' refers to a group of people who identify themselves as belonging to a particular nation group, who are usually ensconced on a particular historical territory, and who have a sense of affinity to people sharing that territory. It is not necessary to specify which traits define a group seeking self-determination.

(Moore, 1997, p.906)

Moore goes on to say, echoing our discussion above, that

> One advantage of conceiving of national identities in subjective terms, and jurisdictional units in terms of the area on which the national group resides, is that it avoids the problem of contested definitions of what really constitutes a nation.

(Moore, 1997, p.907)

We are able to sidestep all such awkward definitional issues and come down to the view that 'Ultimately, communities are nations when a significant percentage of their members think they are nations' (Norman, 1991, p.53). One consequence of this view is that *imagination and symbolism* become essential for defining a nation in the mind of its (potential) members. Before turning to the issue of nationalism as a political ideology, I want to say something brief on this critical point.

> I propose the following definition of the nation: it is an imagined political community. ... It is *imagined* because the members of even the smallest nation will never know most of their fellow-members, meet them, or even hear of them, yet in the minds of each lives the image of their communion.
>
> (Anderson, 1983, pp.5–6)

When it comes to defining a particular nation, potent mixes of historical fact and myth are common: "'to forget and – I will venture to say – to get one's history wrong are essential factors in the making of a nation" [Renan] and "Nationalism requires too much belief in what is patently not so" [Hobsbawm]' (quoted in Archard, 1995, p.472). Beliefs do not need to be true for people to hold to them and act *as if* they were true; 'A group of individuals united in and by the false belief that they share a common history might act collectively and thereby initiate a common history' (Archard, 1995, p.475).

There is plenty of scope for the making of representations, in the form, for example, of constructing and presenting national myths which can be fuel for imagining communities in Anderson's sense. Anderson took the view that 'communities are to be distinguished, not by their falsity/genuineness, but by the style in which they are imagined' (Archard, 1995, p.481). Clearly, not any old claim to nationhood could 'stick' – 'the nation-constituting beliefs must bear some kind of possible relationship to the group of people who are constituted as a nation' (Archard, 1995, p.474) – but would-be nation builders would have plenty of scope to discourage some narratives of nation and to encourage others.

One might argue that a nation not only imagines itself, others imagine it too, and offer constructions or representations of it as a friend or as an enemy. These 'imaginings' matter. Consider, for example, the Israel/Palestine issue. Some Palestinians portray Israel as a tool of Western imperial power in the Middle East, and Israelis protest at such images. On the other hand, consider the argument of the Palestinian critic Edward Said:

> What we must again see is the issue involving *representation*, an issue always lurking near the question of Palestine ... . Zionism always undertakes to speak for Palestine and the Palestinians; this has always meant a blocking operation, by which the Palestinian cannot be heard from (or represent himself) directly on the world stage. Just as the expert Orientalist believed that only he could speak (paternally as it were) for the natives and primitive societies that he had studied – his *presence* denoting their *absence* – so too the Zionists spoke to the world on behalf of the Palestinians.

> (Said, 1979, p.5)

Maps, too, have proven to be a vital part of 'imagining' a nation, in quite a literal sense, creating a visual 'image' of a nation as a state. Maps establish, indeed they create, centres and peripheries, locations and borders, and even the very existence of a political unit. Nation-builders know this fact all too well. For example, in the words of Weizman:

> From 1967 to the present day, Israeli technocrats, ideologues and generals have been drawing maps of the West Bank. Map-making became a national obsession. Whatever the nature of Palestinian spatiality, it was subordinated to Israeli

cartography. Whatever was un-named ceased to exist. Scores of scattered buildings and small villages disappeared from the map, and were never connected to basic services.

(Weizman, 2002)

When one looks more closely at the sheer diversity of those entities that we call 'nations' and 'states', the strong view expressed by anthropologist Clifford Geertz becomes understandable: 'The illusion of a world paved from end to end with repeating units that is produced by the pictorial conventions of our political atlases, polygon cut-outs in a fitted jigsaw, is just that – an illusion' (Geertz, 2000, p.229). Geertz does not deny the material existence of different political systems and the material reality created by the policing of national borders, for example. But he does want us to question whether these separate splashes of colour in atlases really add up to any strong commonalities between the separated political units.

Finally, it is worth pointing out a quite different, provocative perspective that emerges once the symbolic aspects of nation are accepted, as part of a subjective approach to the definition of nations. One could argue that a nation is not something that 'is', but rather it is something that 'does'. What does it mean, what effect is intended or achieved, by calling a group of people a 'nation' (as opposed to a community of some other sort)? Instead of thinking of 'culture' or 'descent', for example, as fixed things, we can ask how different definitions of the nation work or what they accomplish (Verdery, 1996). A nation is a system for classifying people, as are class, gender and so on. We often take these classifications to be 'natural' – 'nation' and 'natural' possess a common etymological root in the sense of 'to be born' – but they can equally be seen as constructed (note the links with the constructivist views of political legitimacy discussed in Chapter 1). Classifications are vital to establishing political centres and peripheries on the ground; they are constructions that do real work, and upon which people act. Notice also how seeing 'nation' as a symbol and a construct makes it a dynamic concept. After all, if 'nation' is a *label*, it can in principle be peeled off one jar and put onto another. There has been talk of the 'Arab nation', for example, over the years, a term used to symbolize a commonality of interest and outlook among Arab peoples regardless of which nation they belong to in the sense of 'nation-state'. A very different example of the dynamism of this label would be the more recent use of the term in the phrase 'queer nation', invoking a sense of commonality among gay communities regardless of what country they are citizens of. This dynamism is clearly one part of what it means for a political idea to be 'living'.

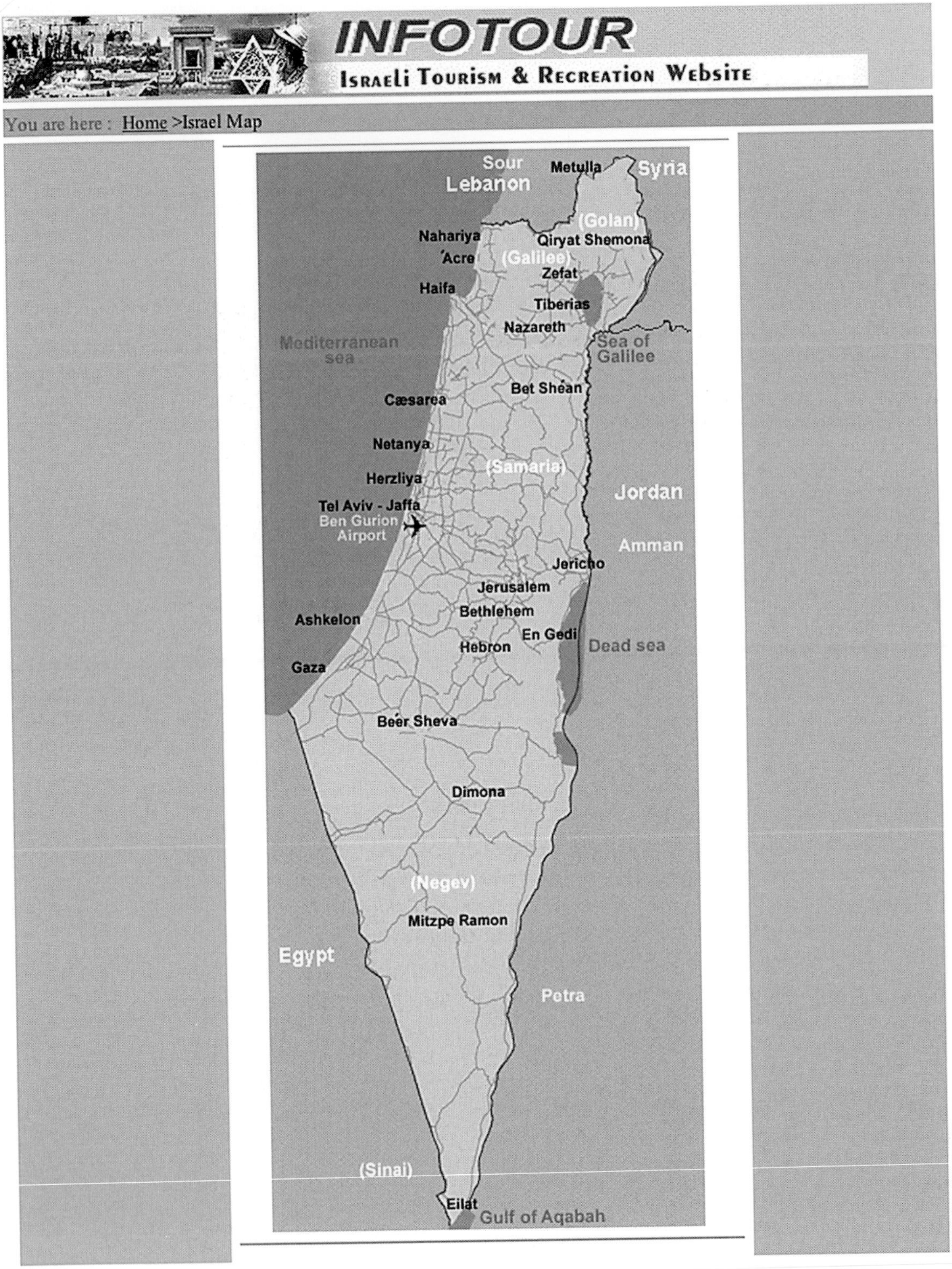

FIGURE 2.3 Visual images of a nation: websites displaying maps for Israeli tourism and depopulated Palestinian villages

PALESTINE FACTS

MAPS

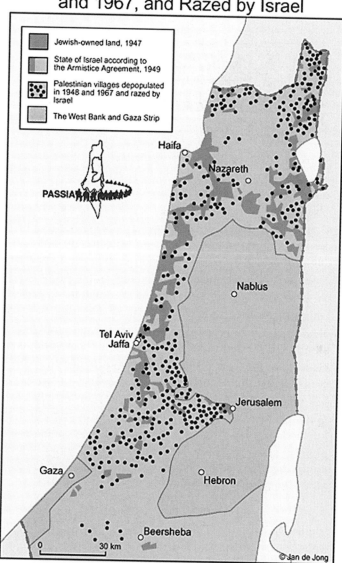

Palestinian Villages Depopulated in 1948 and 1967, and Razed by Israel

Palestinian Academic Society for the Study of International Affairs (PASSIA)

SUMMARY

- There are two main approaches to the definition of nation, the objective approach and the subjective approach.
- The subjective approach is generally favoured by theorists.
- Symbolic and imagined aspects of nationality are important.
- 'Nation' as a word and a label is still evolving, and being applied in new contexts.

5 NATIONALISM AS AN IDEOLOGY

Propagators of ideologies use images and symbols to get people to believe and act in certain ways. Nationalism as a political ideology uses the idea of 'nation' to achieve political goals, and may be the most potent ideology in existence. It is worth reflecting for a moment on what kind of ideology it is. Chapter 1 reminded us that ideology is a contested concept; it is a term that can mean different things. Marx and Engels subscribed to the notion of ideology as a set of ideas that induce false consciousness in workers under capitalism. A second sense of ideology is that set of left and right ideologies we hear about in day-to-day politics: communism, socialism, liberalism and conservatism, for example. Nationalism, we could say, represents a third type of ideology. It is not easy to locate on the left–right 'ideological spectrum', though today nationalist rhetoric, generally speaking, is something more often heard from the political right. It is concerned with creating or maintaining the very political unit that the left–right ideologies *need* to ply their trade in the first place. One could pursue socialist or conservative strategies without reference to national governments, but most often they are thought of, and pursued, in terms of government policies *for* nation-states. So, nationalism is a political ideology, but a distinctive one. In a sense, if a nationalist ideology is successful it *makes possible* the pursuit of other ideologies in the sense of 'left' and 'right' policy prescriptions.

According to Michael Freeden (1998, pp.751–2), whose influential work on ideology is also discussed in Chapters 3 and 5, the five elements which constitute the core structure of nationalism are:

1 'the prioritization of a particular group – the *nation* – as a key constituting and identifying framework for human beings and their practices'

2 'a *positive valorization* is assigned to one's own nation, granting it specific claims over the conduct of its members'

3 'the desire to give *politico-institutional* expression to the first two core concepts'

4 '*space* and *time* are considered to be crucial determinants of social identity'

5 'a sense of belonging and membership in which *sentiment* and *emotion* play an important role'.

Freeden does not discuss explicitly issues of centre and periphery, but notice how the imagining, creation and institutionalizing of centre–periphery relations is critical in this account. The second point puts forward one's nation as a core of value; the third is about the creation of varied markers of centre and periphery; borders, government institutions and others that embody, and which make real, what the ideology has imagined.

Freeden rightly warns that this set of concepts cannot be used to explain a great deal in itself. It is necessarily a highly abstract set of elements, which need filling out with particularities of specific cases and elaboration using other concepts. Nevertheless it provides a useful frame for exploring the texture of nationalism as an ideology. We will consider four of these elements in turn (discussion of space and time, the fourth element, is implicitly covered in the discussion of the others).

I 'The prioritization of a particular group – the *nation* – as a key constituting and identifying framework for human beings and their practices'

No *particular* form of articulating the nation is required by the formulation of this first element; the nation might be 'imagined' or 'constructed' as homogenous or as pluralistic and diverse, for example. However nationhood is imagined, though, it will invariably involve some form of suppression of alternative ways of classifying peoples; indeed, just as particular conceptions of 'centre' and 'periphery' can only become dominant by staving off alternative conceptions. Consider that for most of us there are linguistic, class, ethnic, location, gender, religious and other aspects to our identities. If nationalists want to subsume all these under nationality as the primary marker of identity, we might have grounds to suspect the move. Often, observers distinguish liberal nationalism from illiberal nationalism. The former embraces the plurality of the sources of identity, while the latter subsumes other aspects under nationality Consider briefly three alternative ways of constructing or classifying political 'community', which may either cut across or reinforce nationalist classifications:

(a) '*Functional*' *communities*. People often identify with functional rather than territorial groups. Class solidarities, for example, which arise from people's positions within the relations of production of a country (or a region, or indeed within the global economy), can and do cut across national and other territorially based solidarities. Marx, to cite the most prominent example, knew this well: 'Workers of the world unite!' was precisely a call for workers everywhere to unite against the exploitative conditions they shared, regardless of national or other attachments.

(b) *Religious communities.* Religion can operate like class in that it can establish and activate loyalties that owe little or nothing to territorial location or boundaries. Often a dimension of time and circumstance can transform religion, along with gender and class for example, from a subversive to a reinforcing element within nationalist discourses. In the Algerian war of independence from France in the late 1950s, for example, Islam was undoubtedly a reinforcing element within Algerian nationalism, albeit largely secondary to the secular and socialist character of the main liberation movement, the FLN. More recently, with the resurgence of a particular form of political Islam – another ideology, relatively recent on the global scene and powerfully important in the wake of '9-11' – against the perceived corruptions of the governments of Algeria and a number of other Arab states, a particular interpretation of one religion has become a deeply subversive element.

(c) *Regional and global community?* It is a source of irony for some commentators that a resurgence of nationalism after the collapse of communism in Russia and in Eastern Europe has come at a time when the primacy of the nation-state in some key respects is being challenged by something called 'globalization' (see **Gieben and Lewis, 2005**; **Guibernau, 2005**). According to some influential views, globalization does involve large-scale trends which add up to a significant challenge to our dominant national conceptions of political community. David Held (2000) has recommended that we adapt democracy so that new 'constituencies' that cross national boundaries can be recognized and their members participate

FIGURE 2.4 Celebration of a nation: Bangladeshi women parade at a ceremony celebrating the thirtieth anniversary of the declaration of independence from Pakistan, March 2001

in decision making on cross-border issues. He and others have also advocated global government through a world parliament and other institutions. Such views see the community as made up of those *affected by* certain actions or phenomena, *regardless* of their territorial location and loyalties. It is people affected by, for example, AIDS, acid rain and global warming, who form a new sort of 'constituency' and a new type of collective interest. The concern here is about people in different countries, drawn together in new forms of 'political community' by having a stake in the outcome of pressing cross-border issues, and the need to downgrade more rigidly national-territorial (and to some degree also legal) definitions of political community.

2   'A *positive valorization* is assigned to one's own nation, granting it specific claims over the conduct of its members'

Just how a nation is prioritized over other communities will have an important impact on how the terms of this second element are played out. A nation that sees itself in pluralistic or liberal terms for example – which may celebrate cultural diversity as part of its very sense of a collective identity – is, on the face of it, less likely to make particular demands or to institute extensive controls on the behaviour of its members. On the other hand, a nation that is imagined in terms of the more monolithic view of a more homogenous culture will be more likely to be directive in its treatment of its members. Apart from 'loyalty demands', valorization may also encompass 'superiority claims' which hold that other peoples, ethnic groups or nations are inferior in some respect. There is no *necessary* connection between racism and nationalism. Recent nationalist trends in the older democracies of Europe – the success of *Front Nationale* leader Jean-Marie Le Pen in becoming one of the final two candidates in the run-off for the French presidency in 2002, and the rise in votes for the far right in Switzerland, Austria, Denmark, Belgium and The Netherlands – do hint at or openly articulate such claims. More progressive forms of nationalism, which were more common throughout the process of decolonization in the twentieth century, generally did not do so.

3   'The desire to give *politico-institutional* expression to the first two core concepts'

There is a strong case for regarding the third element in the 'core structure' of nationalism as the key one. Generally, as we have seen, nationalists want their nation to have a state, or statehood. But political self-determination might have other outlets.

From the comparatively 'soft' demands to harder and less compromising ones, the spectrum might consist of some form of:

- *recognition* of the cultural distinctiveness of a 'national' minority community within a state, accompanied by institutions (cultural councils, a dedicated ministry, and so on) which sponsor the interests of that group (think of the 'first nations' in Canada)

- *cultural federalism*, where specific functions such as education are handed over to recognized 'national' or cultural groups for them to run on a semi-autonomous basis within an existing state
- *regional federalism*, where a territorial group has the right to run its own affairs substantially within a particular location within the state
- embryonic and possibly transitory *'statehood'* which might not be territorially continuous but may involve the promise of substantial degrees of autonomy (as with the current Palestinian Authority)
- embryonic statehood under temporary international (normally UN) tutelage and protection, as in East Timor and Kosovo in recent years after the violent conflicts in both places
- full independent statehood and recognition as such from other states and international bodies.

Different demands for national self-determination could lead to any one of these, or a combination of them. Some commentators are wary that demands for strong forms of national self-determination might be met (by colonial powers for example) with co-optive strategies, offering a lesser degree of autonomy in the hope of buying off or defusing the autonomy demands. Avner De-Shalit, for example, makes the point that the demand for self-determination is a *political* and not a *cultural* demand. Discussing the case of Palestine, he makes the case that cultural autonomy would not be enough to satisfy Palestinian demands, in theory or in practice:

> Autonomy may be the solution to something but not to the Palestinian demand for national self-determination. The demand is political, and it therefore requires free institutions and a grass-roots democracy with active and meaningful participation, enabling Palestinians to determine their own rules, form independent foreign relationships, do business using their own currency, and have their own history of independence. All this is lacking in the solution of autonomy.
>
> (De-Shalit, 1996, p.916)

The importance of 'giving expression' to the political aspirations of one's own nation is clearly evident in how important the 'trappings of statehood' are – to aspiring states and existing ones. Consider, for example, disputes over the draft constitution of the EU in 2003 (the constitution was signed by European leaders in October 2004). The UK government was concerned about its sovereign statehood, and sought to expunge the word 'federal' from the draft, which included the statement that the EU 'shall administer certain common competences on a federal basis' (cited in Castle, 2003). Federalism does imply decentralization, which is why many other countries in the EU don't mind it. But it *also* implies that the EU would be a state-like entity, despite policy decentralization. For the UK government it was a challenge to the notion of the EU as a union of states. Giving expression to one's nation can stretch to *retaining* expression of those things that make it a nation-state. Prime Minister Tony Blair made this clear at the EU summit set up to finalize the new constitution when he said:

Of particular importance to us is the recognition – expressly – that what we want is a Europe of nations, not a federal superstate. ... Taxation, foreign policy, defence policy and our own British borders will remain the prerogative of our national government and national Parliament. That is immensely important.

(Black and White, 2003)

To the Palestinians, for example, the trappings of statehood are vital from a quite different angle. Presenting the 'halfway-house' institutions of the Palestinian Authority as a sort of embryonic statehood has been important. As the post-Iraqi war context led to the US-sponsored 'road map' for Middle East peace, there was a sense that 'Palestine' both exists as a political entity – as a 'state', to be more precise – *and* that it did not. There is a 'Palestinian Authority' (though not called a 'government'); and there is a 'Palestinian Legislative Council' (though it is often referred to as a 'quasi-parliament', implying that it is not a *real* parliament, i.e. part of a real government of a real state). The late Palestinian leader Yasser Arafat had the 'chairmanship' of the PA, but he was not a 'president'. But the PA does have a 'Prime Minister' – a position occupied since its inception in 2003 by Mahmoud Abbas and then Ahmed Qureia. Here we have a desire on the part of Palestinians and the other sponsors of the peace process to name and operate institutions and offices which look and sound state-like.

5 'A sense of belonging and membership in which *sentiment* and *emotion* play an important role'

Nationalism is about land or territory and what it means to people. Nationalists make claims to the centrality of certain tracts of land to them, to their people, to their collective history, traditions, cultures and sufferings:

When a hundred thousand nationalists march down Sherbrooke Street [in Montreal] chanting 'Le Quebec aux Quebecois', they are not just talking about the establishment of a public language or about the protection of Quebecois culture. They are talking about a whole relation between a people and a territory and the future.

(Walker, 1999, p.155)

Emotional attachment to land takes on various shades in debates about nationality and community. As we have seen, it is material, economic and symbolic, all at once. It is about ownership and appropriation, inclusion of one's own nation and exclusion of others. *Naming* is a critical part of this, a fact that is clear in the example of the Palestinian–Israeli conflict:

Some Arab villages in pre-1948 Palestine that were abandoned during the 1948 War were renamed with Hebrew equivalents leading to contestations over municipal rights; the Arab village of Ein Houd, for instance, was re-established in 1953 as the Israeli artists' colony Ein Hod.

(Sucharov, 1999, p.185)

Indeed, more generally, attachment to land, and imbuing of land with loaded symbolic meanings, is a core aspect of this conflict. Palestinians (and all Arabs), for example, call Jerusalem *al-Qods*, which translates as 'the holy', imbuing the city with special spiritual–political significance; a spiritual as well as a political and geographical *centre* of Palestine. Similarly,

> To nurture their historic claim to Zion throughout the centuries, Jews have had to call up historical narratives and national symbols to strengthen the imagined link between the people and the land. Jews have historically sung folk songs about returning to Zion, and the Jewish liturgy contains references to the sanctity of Jerusalem and the land.

(Sucharov, 1999, p.186)

Note too that borders and boundaries do not have to be understood as they normally are: fixed entities with clear meanings and consequences. Recent analyses, for example, have explored national boundaries as 'complicated social processes and discourses rather than fixed lines' (Paasi, 1999, p.73). One can argue that boundaries do not persist by virtue of their being drawn on agreed maps, but primarily through daily practices which enact and reinforce them; from checkpoint controls to signs, for example. Further, our notion of what really constitutes 'boundaries' needs to be flexible to capture a raft of daily political realities, as the work of **Huysmans (2005)** with respect to asylum seeking testifies. In a similar vein, but in a very different context, consider what historian Rashid Khalidi calls 'the quintessential Palestinian experience', which 'illustrates some of the most basic issues raised by Palestinian identity' ... [and which] takes place at a border, an airport, a checkpoint: in short, at any one of those many modern barriers where

identities are checked and verified. What happens to Palestinians at these crossing points brings home to them how much they share in common as a people' (Khalidi, 1997, p.1).

In this section we have explored the different dimensions of nationalism as an ideology. We now turn to ways in which political theorists have tried to deal with the issue of principles for national self-determination and secession.

SUMMARY

- Nationalism is a particularly potent ideology, arguably different from other forms of ideology.
- Freeden sets out various elements of the core structure of nationalism, which help to frame debates about and discussions of the idea and its practice.

6 NATIONAL SELF-DETERMINATION: WHEN IS SECESSION JUSTIFIED?

By valuing a group positively and seeking self-determination for it, nationalists often set out to redraw maps, to create new countries or to reinstate old ones. It is rare for this to occur without (often violent) conflict. Can political theorists offer guides to dealing peacefully with such disputes?

One question which political theorists have focused on has been that of secession. Secession as an issue carries with it most of the dilemmas associated with nations and nationalism, and whether theorists can say anything useful in terms of rights and wrongs. In cases of dispute, how might one decide which communities should be self-governing?

Surprisingly few political theorists have paid sustained attention to this problem. One exception has been Frederick Whelan, whose search for a satisfactory guiding principle ended in a pessimism that is evident when he writes that: 'it appears that our only choices are to abide by the arbitrary verdicts of history or war, or to appeal on an ad hoc basis to other principles, none of which commands general respect' (Whelan, 1983, p.16). Nevertheless, vigorous debate continues. Let's map some of the approaches theorists have taken.

Consider a country we can call 'Y', which consists of three different groups: the As, the Bs and the Cs. The most numerous group are the As, making up 60 per cent of the population. The Bs make up 30 per cent and the Cs 10 per cent. We could look at country Y and ask: which communities should be self-determining here?

The first response might be that it simply does not matter as long as country Y is democratically governed. Separating out or combining together different cultural communities makes no difference because if the state is democratic everyone has full rights to liberty and basic equalities anyway. This is a provocative view, one that liberals (who see people as essentially the same underneath their outward differences) often find attractive. But the fact is that people do feel identification with others, and often wish to be governed with, and by, particular others, people from 'their' group. As we have seen, the recasting of the world political map after the end of the Cold War forced many more theorists to address issues of nationalism and community.

A second response might be to find objective criteria to distinguish one political community from another, and apply them. But we have seen the very real difficulties in trying to construct 'objective' indices.

So what other approaches are there if we accept that the issue can't be ignored, and that we need to take a subjective approach to it? A more promising third response among advocates of democracy has been to search for *democratic* answers to these dilemmas. We could ignore democratic mechanisms and just say 'leave it up to the people in Y, they'll work it out'. But we would be right to be wary of coercive means (such as 'ethnic cleansing') to determine which political communities should be self-governing.

Democracy is often taken to mean 'majority rule', or sometimes 'majority rule, minority rights'. Often, however, writers on the subject have ignored the prior question; 'majority of *which* group of people?' We are caught in a vicious circle, it seems, where the people cannot decide who are 'the people' (or who constitutes 'the nation') until we know who the people are who can decide!

Some theorists have suggested ways out of this vicious circle. Consider country Y again. If groups A, B and C are all governed within Y as one state, and there is no significant dispute about the legitimacy of Y, then issues do not arise. But what if Bs want to secede and form their own state? What could make their secession legitimate?

The democratic theorist will answer: democratic majorities. So if a majority of people in B vote for an independent state, it should be granted. Democratic theorist Robert A. Dahl emphasizes the point that the would-be new state should itself be a democracy, and most would be happy to add that criterion (Dahl, 1989). But again, there are some tough questions that need to be addressed.

1 *Who should get to vote on secession?*

The Bs (encompassing the Cs) or all the As too? After all, democracy is often said to be about people who are affected by an issue having a say on it; and As will certainly be affected if Bs secede. This is a live issue with regard to Northern Ireland's future, for example. If a referendum were to decide if the province should join the Irish Republic, should the voters include all UK voters and all Irish voters, or just those living in the province? If, for example, there were to be a vote on the creation of an independent Palestinian state, what would be the appropriate constituency: (a) Palestinians living in the occupied territories, which might become the state, or (b) these plus Palestinians living elsewhere (the 'diaspora'), and/or (c) those living in the occupied territories plus Israeli citizens? Clearly, the answers to these questions are politically critical.

One writer on secession, Harry Beran, has proposed that there should be a *series* of votes in such difficult cases. The proposed boundaries of a would-be new state could be expanded or contracted slightly from one vote to the next. The idea is to maximize the number of people who live in a political community of their choosing. For example, if some of the people of Northern Ireland wanted to vote to leave the UK and join the Irish Republic, a series of votes could be held on the issue. In each subsequent vote, the boundaries around the voting group could be expanded or (normally) contracted in order to maximize the percentage of people desiring the change. But while this 'solution' might maximize the number of people being able to belong where they choose, it does have its problems. One is that in principle it favours secessionists over integrationists, whereas there may be reasons not to allow the stability of existing arrangements to be upset so fundamentally. Perhaps more importantly, it may only work well where a would-be secessionist group occupies a continuous slice of territory. Where a group is interspersed among others who do not wish to change the status quo, the dangerous spectre of significant and forced population movements raises its head. The deaths as people moved east and west with the creation of Pakistan in 1949 offer a stark reminder of those potential dangers.

2   *What size of majority vote should decide the issue?*

In many types of democratic vote, a bare majority (technically, 50 per cent +1) is enough to decide outcomes. But often constitutional changes – changes which would affect the basic structures or political rules of the game – are regarded as needing 'supermajorities' of, say, 60 or 70 per cent. A basic change in the sovereign political unit would certainly count as a constitutional change. If the Bs get to vote, we might be concerned if only a bare majority favoured secession, especially if the voting turnout was low. Because the Cs form a minority within the B community, should we look for a majority of Cs as well? In addition, the turnout might be a special issue for such significant constitutional changes.

3   *Does one community seceding grant a similar right to others?*

Consider the position of community C. If B secedes, it takes C with it into the new state. But does C then have the same right to secede from B? Consider the case of Quebec. In the most recent independence referendum, Quebecois separatists came very close to achieving the bare majority they need to achieve their goal. But if they have the right to secede from Canada, would other groups who do not see themselves as a part of a francophone entity likewise have the right to a further independence vote for themselves? What about non-francophone immigrant communities, or indigenous 'nations', within Quebec? If one secession, democratically sanctioned, is acceptable, then why not other, subsequent or consequent ones? Some theorists who broadly accept a democratic model of secession still worry about a 'domino effect', where one secession will provoke others, and we will end up with a patchwork quilt of ever-smaller political units (or countries). I return in a moment to the question of whether there are good reasons for us to be so concerned about the size of nation-states.

4 *Do our answers depend on who the groups are?*

Finally, perhaps our intuition about how to deal democratically with country Y depends on who we think the As, Bs and Cs are. Consider three possibilities:
(i) A is the UK, B is Scotland, C is the Shetland Islands
(ii) A is the EU, B is the UK, C is Scotland
(iii) A is a world government, B is the EU, C is France.

Does your intuition about the rights of communities A, B and C shift from case to case? If so, is the shift due to a reflex to favour the sovereign, self-governing status of existing nation-states? Or is it because you favour decentralization in principle, or because you are an advocate of 'ever closer union' in the EU, or indeed of world government? Perhaps exploring our intuition in this way tells us something about the uses and limits of political theory. We must be careful to examine the assumptions we bring to our analyses, and be sensitive to the assumptions of the theorists we read.

5 *What about a more restrictive 'remedial right?'*

Some theorists, such as Allen Buchanan, favour placing higher hurdles in the path of would-be secessionist movements. Rather than endorsing some rather permissive form of democratic right to national self-determination, he favours a more restrictive remedial right. Only those 'national' groups who can show that they suffer systematic historical injustice, or have so suffered, have a strong case for independent statehood. In one sense, this approach takes us full circle; if there is no great injustice, and if a minority 'national' community (Bs or Cs, for example, in country Y) is governed in a largely democratic manner, then we ought to favour the status quo.

6 *What about alternatives to secession?*

We have seen that in principle there are alternatives: cultural autonomy or a form of federalism. There are alternative ways to delineate political centres and peripheries apart from full secession.

One conclusion to arise from this discussion of secession is that we are not cast adrift without any general principles or guidelines. We have also seen how the complexities of the real political world impinge upon political theories, and how those theories in turn can help us to make sense of the world. This is a core aspect of what it means to examine 'living' political ideas. Debates among theorists about secession may highlight how worried these theorists are about *nationalism*. There are versions and examples of nationalism which are anything but liberal and tolerant of others (perhaps Serbian nationalism is a contemporary example). There are others where, arguably, the opposite seems to be the case (Scottish or Quebecois nationalism might be examples). Looked at through the lens of illiberal nationalism, 'permissive' theories of secession, like the stronger democratic theories we looked at, may raise concerns. After all, the democratic theories may end up endorsing either ethnic cleansing or systematic colonization. The ethnic cleansing involved in efforts to create 'Republic Serbska' in Bosnia in the early 1990s would be an example of the former strategy. The moving of Moroccans into the western Sahara since 1974, and constantly putting off the day of an independence referendum for that region as the population changes in a more congenial direction, might be seen as an example of the second. Faced with these sorts of possibilities, we might be moved to favour 'high hurdle' theories of secession instead (Beiner, 2003), such as the remedial approach.

However, the issue might look different when viewed through the lens of liberal nationalism. If we take a broadly positive view of nationalist movements that are largely democratic and respectful of minorities, then the more permissive democratic approach may be more appealing. Again, there are important lessons here about the relationship between political theory and political practice. Even in cases where theories come across as abstract and general, assumptions about the real political world can and will influence our approaches.

There are no easy answers to the adequacy of secession and referendums as tools for the satisfaction of claims to national self-determination. Each case will throw up unique features; political theory cannot simply provide a universal blueprint for dealing with such specific claims. Having said that, perhaps it is the case that 'democracy' is not just a matter of votes, for instance in secession referendums. It has been suggested that we may be able to take all the concerns about multiple claims for self-determination – illiberal nationalism, the domino effect, political instability and so on – and incorporate them into a wider approach to 'democratic management' of these issues: 'the project of democratic management must protect minorities, resist majority tyranny, correct the misuse of majority rule, and achieve a workable balance between majority rule and minority rights' (Baogang He, 2002, p.93).

We noted in passing that some observers worry about permissive approaches to national self-determination and secession, on the grounds that we would end up with a patchwork of too many small states. Critics are concerned about the potential destabilizing effects of a secessionist free-for-all. Many larger states today are not in fact national states, but rather multinational states. Encouraging national self-determination in a strong and literal way might threaten the integrity of all but a handful of the world's existing states:

> Is it theoretically coherent to try to apply the self-determination principle to *all* multinational or multiethnic states? ... Carried to the logical limit, the theoretical consequences are somewhat catastrophic; for hardly any states today would be immune from having their legitimacy normatively subverted.
>
> (Beiner, 1999, p.5)

In a similar vein, Ernest Gellner once wrote that we live in a world that 'has only space for something of the order of 200 or 300 national states' (quoted in Beiner, 1999, p.5). Leaving aside the fact that a world of 300 states would be enormously different from one with the almost 200 states of today, there is a case for replying to this by pointing out that size is quite arbitrary when it comes to nation-states. This issue much exercised the great democratic theorists around the time of the American and French Revolutions. Putting it simply, the terms of the debate can be seen as being set by Jean-Jacques Rousseau, the famous Swiss-French political theorist and an inspiration for the French Revolution, who felt that liberty was threatened whenever a political unit grew beyond the size of a city-state; and James Madison, American revolutionary and the fourth president of the USA, who saw the extension of the political unit to continental proportions as a positive barrier to factional domination of a political system.

There are two basic ways in which we can understand the question of the appropriate size of political units. The first is to interpret it as a question about the appropriate extent of a unit's geographical area. The second is to see it as a question about the size of the population of the unit. Geographical size is, arguably, less significant now than before the communications revolution. Peripheral regions of a large political unit need not be out of touch with activities at the centre. Political participation, especially in elections, is not unduly hampered by distances. The question of population size may be more important. Robert A. Dahl suggests that the 'smaller is better' argument looks ridiculous if pushed to extremes: 'If it were true that a smaller system must always be more democratic than a larger, then the most democratic system would consist of one person, which would be absurd' (Dahl, 1989, p.205). But there is little need to jump to such extremes. A further objection to the argument that smaller is better is Dahl's view that larger units allow for citizens to have some say in more matters. In other words, the scope of policy in larger units is greater; citizens can participate in the resolution of more issues than they could in smaller units. This may be true, but those 'extra' things one might be able to influence may not be matters which citizens are generally concerned about.

Further, the objects of citizen concern can be as much the *product* of the very existence of the larger unit. For example, the USA being a larger unit means that citizens can have some (highly indirect and minimal) say in nuclear weapons policies, clearly a matter of global importance. However, it is arguably the existence of political units of such continental dimensions which has generated the resources to devote to such weapons in the first place. Smaller units may restrict citizens' say to smaller, more local matters, but in a world of smaller units the global questions may not loom so large anyway; these small, local matters would no longer seem, or even be, small or merely local.

SUMMARY

- The issue of secession has proved to be a challenge to political theory, and shows how practice impinges on theory.

- A series of referendums, or 'remedial right', are two prominent approaches to secession.

- Attitudes to nationalism are influenced by whether a given example is seen as 'liberal' or 'illiberal'.

- The question of the appropriate size of political units is part of debates on nationalism.

7 CONCLUSION

We have explored nations, national self-determination and secession as living political ideas. Perhaps the key points to emerge from the discussion are that:

- the nation-state is the basic political community in the contemporary world, despite regional and global challenges

- subjective approaches to defining nations, prioritizing awareness of belonging to a national group, have advantages over efforts to construct objective definitions

- the symbolic, imagined, aspects of nations can be as important as historical or other cultural 'facts' about the nation

- nationalism is a many-sided and potent political ideology, though we can pinpoint some general characteristics shared by all nationalist movements

- political theorists have offered imaginative responses to dilemmas of secession and national self-determination, such as the democratic and remedial approaches

- all theoretical 'solutions' to issues of secession are vulnerable to objections

- our assessments of political theories can depend on (sometimes unspoken) assumptions that we make about political realities and specific cases.

REFERENCES

Anderson, B. (1983) *Imagined Communities: Reflections on the Origin and Spread of Nationalism*, London, Verso.

Archard, D. (1995) 'Myths, lies and historical truth: a defence of nationalism', *Political Studies*, vol.43, no.3.

Baogang He (2002) 'Referenda as a solution to the national-identity/boundary question: an empirical critique of the theoretical literature', *Alternatives*, vol.27.

Beiner, R. (1999) 'Introduction: nationalism's challenge to political philosophy' in Beiner, R. (ed.).

Beiner, R. (2003) 'Review of Moore, M., *The Ethnics of Nationalism*', *Ethics*, January.

Beiner, R. (ed.) (1999) *Theorizing Nationalism*, New York, SUNY Press.

Black, I. and White, M. (2003) 'Giscard's warning: don't tamper with my EU draft', *The Guardian*, 21 June.

Castle, S. (2003) 'EU blueprint drops federal reference after Blair protests', *The Independent*, 24 May.

Charlesworth, J. and Humphreys, W. (2005) 'Challenging centre–periphery relations in health policy' in Prokhovnik, R. (ed.) *Making Policy, Shaping Lives*, Edinburgh, Edinburgh University Press/The Open University.

Dahl, R.A. (1989) *Democracy and Its Critics*, New Haven, Yale University Press.

De-Shalit, A. (1996) 'National self-determination: political not cultural', *Political Studies*, vol.44, no.5.

Freeden, M. (1998) 'Is nationalism a distinct ideology?', *Political Studies*, vol.46, no.4.

Geertz, C. (2000) *Available Light: Anthropological Reflections on Philosophical Topics*, Princeton, Princeton University Press.

Gieben, B. and Lewis, P. (2005) 'Framing politics: the state in context' in Lewis, P. (ed.) *Exploring Political Worlds*, Edinburgh, Edinburgh University Press/The Open University.

Guibernau, M. (1996) *Nationalisms*, Cambridge, Polity Press.

Guibernau, M. (2005) 'Centre–periphery relations: government beyond Westminster' in Heffernan, R. and Thompson, G.F. (eds).

Heffernan, R. and Thompson, G.F. (eds) (2005) *Politics and Power in the UK*, Edinburgh, Edinburgh University Press/The Open University.

Held, D. (2000) 'The changing contours of political community: rethinking democracy in the context of globalization' in Holden, B.B. (ed.) *Global Democracy: a Debate*, London, Routledge.

Huysmans, J. (2005) *What is Politics?*, Edinburgh, Edinburgh University Press/The Open University.

Khalidi, R. (1997) *Palestinian Identity: the Construction of Modern National Consciousness*, New York, Columbia University Press.

Moore, M. (1997) 'On national self-determination', *Political Studies*, vol.45, no.5.

Newman, D. (ed.) (1999) *Boundaries, Territory and Postmodernity*, London, Frank Cass.

Norman, W. (1999) 'Theorizing nationalism (normatively)' in Beiner, R. (ed.).

Paasi, A. (1999) 'Boundaries as social processes: territoriality in the world of flows' in Newman, D. (ed.).

Said, E. (1979) *The Question of Palestine*, London, Routledge and Kegan Paul.

Sucharov, M. (1999) 'Regional identity and the sovereignty principle: explaining Israeli–Palestinian peacemaking' in Newman, D. (ed.).

Thompson, G.F. (2005) 'Policy networks and interest representation' in Heffernan, R. and Thompson, G.F. (eds).

Verdery, K. (1996) 'Whither "nation" and "nationalism"?' in Balakrishnan, G. (ed.) *Mapping the Nation*, London, Verso.

Walker, B. (1999) 'Modernity and cultural vulnerability: should ethnicity be privileged?' in Beiner, R. (ed.).

Weizman, E. (2002) 'The politics of verticality', http://opendemocracy.net/dynamics/dynamic_website_document.asp?DocID=1254&Action=DisplayPage (accessed 10 May 2002).

Whelan, F. (1983) 'Prologue: democratic theory and the boundary problem' in Pennock, J.R. and Chapman, R.W. (eds) *Nomos XXV: Liberal Democracy*, New York, New York University Press.

FURTHER READING

Anderson, B. (1983) *Imagined Communities: Reflections on the Origin and Spread of Nationalism*, London, Verso.

Beiner, R. (ed.) (1999) *Theorizing Nationalism*, New York, SUNY Press.

Freeden, M. (1998) 'Is nationalism a distinct ideology?', *Political Studies*, vol.46, no.4.

Dissent and the re-invention of politics

Geoff Andrews

Participation & dissent

Contents

1 INTRODUCTION

It might seem odd to think of dissent as being essential to the practice of politics. For one thing it is often seen as 'on the margins' of politics, carried out by those seeking to disrupt or abstain from the political system, to cause trouble or be 'awkward'. Dissenters or 'dissidents' as they are usually known, are often seen in negative terms as not playing the game or who, following (Groucho) Marx, refuse to join any group which would accept them as members. In some societies, to express dissent is a life and death issue or one which has cost dissidents prolonged loss of freedom. In liberal democratic societies, such as the contemporary UK, questions of dissent do not have the same implications. Yet, here too, whether it is the state taking on greater powers of surveillance, such as monitoring emails, or political parties going to great lengths to ensure that their representatives all sing from the same hymn sheet, dissent is still often frowned upon.

Yet dissent has always been a crucial element of politics and dissidents have often been in the forefront of social and political change. In the cases of Nelson Mandela and Vaclav Havel, the transition from dissident (including long spells in jail) to statesman by the beginning of the 1990s illustrates the role dissent can have in influencing political change. In this way it can be a force for 're-inventing politics' through, in this case, major political transformation. Mandela and Havel did not act alone; they were leaders of dissident movements and groups of intellectuals, the African National Congress and Charter 77 (and later Civic Forum), respectively. Both were banned organizations in the two countries concerned, apartheid South Africa and communist Czechoslovakia.

Members of these organizations did not have the right to exercise legitimate dissent and had to organize underground as clandestine networks. That is, they had to express their dissent outside mainstream political structures and without the rights of free citizens. Their status as dissidents and the implications of their dissent are clear to see. However, the case of dissidents in liberal democratic societies, where rights to freedom of expression do exist, is more complex. Noam Chomsky, for example, a long-standing dissident and critic of foreign policy in the USA, does not face the restrictions of Mandela or Havel. Yet he would claim that there are clear attempts to suppress his views as well as other dissident voices. During the Iraq war in 2003, opponents of the war were kept off the air of public broadcasting in the USA, on the basis that the morale of the troops would be undermined. This suggests that democratic societies at certain times – often driven by what governments perceive as the 'national interest' or issues of 'national security' – also impose severe constraints on dissent.

Therefore, one starting point in any discussion of dissent is the need to recognize that as a particular type of political participation, dissent has taken on different forms at different times in different political systems. Moreover, to ask what it means to be a dissident is to open up a whole set of questions about the nature of politics itself. For example, we would need to know about the distribution of power, about the rights to freedom of speech and association, the political system and the constitutional arrangements that exist before we arrive at any understanding. We would also need to know about the political ideologies that have helped shape political systems and in particular the way in which the meaning of dissent has been conditioned and constrained by them. In this respect we need to understand dissent as a living political idea, which takes on different meanings and is often contested, according to rival political interpretations. For example, it is unlikely that any political belief system would propose unlimited dissent. The important question therefore becomes: what are the appropriate boundaries and constraints on the nature and extent of dissent? In addressing this question we need to draw on traditions of political thought, debates among political

thinkers, the work of political theorists and the ideological world of the dissident. As a living political idea, dissent will allow us in this chapter to open up a deeper analysis of the role ideas play in politics and, through the examples that follow, an evaluation of the way in which ideologies 'work' – as 'vehicles of dissent'.

As well as being a living political idea with its own history dissent, as is the case with self-determination and social justice discussed in other chapters in this book, should also be considered as a political *concept*. As such, it is an analytical tool used by political theorists in their attempts to construct a normative outline of how political society should be organized. In Chapter 4 in this volume, David Middleton shows how social justice provides a similar role for political theorists such as Rawls, in their attempts to set out a *fair* social and political order, while in Vivienne Brown's Chapter 1, we have seen the way in which *political obligation* was crucial in the work of theorists such as Hobbes and Locke, in the construction of their respective civic orders. In the previous chapter Michael Saward explained how *self-determination* was vital to the design of a democratic and independent polity. This should not mean that these concepts have a fixed or static meaning, applicable in all times and places. Different political cultures and models of democracy carry their own particular 'discourses' of dissent which have shaped and constrained its meanings and application. Indeed, one of the purposes of this book is to show the ways in which political theories are themselves influenced by political change, ideological debate and historical contexts.

This chapter will therefore discuss the meanings and applications of dissent and, through the example of the 'British Enlightenment', also look at the way dissent developed as a living political idea crucial to the development of modern British politics. Then, it will go on to discuss the status of dissent as a political concept, namely an analytical tool used by political theorists to interpret the political world. Finally, situating dissent within the context of political ideology, the chapter will argue that dissent is crucial to the renewal and reinvention of politics.

2 DIMENSIONS OF DISSENT

While keeping the different *definitional* criteria in mind, we also need to *classify* political dissent. In other words, what do we mean when we describe a political act as one of dissent? How might it differ, for example, from political opposition? Here we can distinguish between two broad dimensions, namely those acts of dissent which challenge the legitimacy of the state (including its laws) or those which object to dominant political values. In the first of these dimensions it would include, for example, questioning the legitimacy of certain laws on moral or political grounds. This might be through acts of civil disobedience, that is principled actions of law-breaking, such as blocking the roads to raise awareness of the needs of disabled people, or occupying empty houses to draw attention to the plight of the homeless. Civil disobedience, as a method used by dissidents, has a long tradition in politics and is distinct from criminal acts of law-breaking where the motives are for individual or selfish ends. It has been the method used by many activists in what are called 'acts of conscience', whereby moral grounds are used to challenge a law or state policy. Dissidents who have used these methods include Mahatma Gandhi, in his passive resistance to British rule in India, and the suffragettes, who chained themselves to the railings of the British parliament while campaigning for votes for women in the first part of the last century.

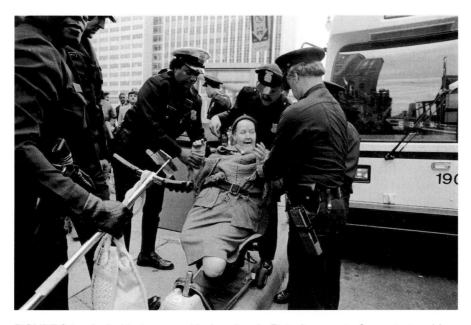

FIGURE 3.1   A disabled woman blocks a bus in Detroit as part of a protest and is arrested by police

The second dimension of dissent is the questioning of dominant values by dissidents who believe that such values have reinforced discrimination or have led to other forms of social conflict or division. In doing so this form of dissent also brings existing power relations into question. Feminist campaigns against perceived 'sexist' portrayal of women in adverts would be one example, on the basis that such advertisements reflect patriarchal assumptions, thereby legitimizing the subordination of women. Another example here would be Mary Whitehouse's Viewers and Listeners Association which, from the 1960s, sought public disagreement with the pervasiveness of the ideas of the so-called 'permissive society', which amongst other things (it was claimed) served to undermine the traditional family. It is important to keep in mind that the differences between these two dimensions of dissent are not always clear-cut and there are many examples which include aspects of both elements. For example, members of the gay and lesbian group Outrage have challenged what they perceived as the unfairness of laws governing the age of consent, as well as the pervasiveness of heterosexuality as a set of dominant values in structuring social life and reinforcing stereotypes. The distinction is useful, however, in helping us to assess and classify different types of dissent and subsequently to assess their merit.

The examples of the Viewers and Listeners Association and Outrage illustrate the varied and transient nature of dissent. In other words how we classify dissent depends on an understanding of the dynamics of political change. We must recognize that dissidents belong to both left and right of the political spectrum, while yesterday's mainstream politician can become tomorrow's dissident. At the start of the 1990s, the Conservative politician, Norman Tebbit, was at the heart of government and championed as the representative of the 'man in the street'; by the end of that decade, the views he espoused (his rejection of multiculturalism in particular) were regarded as that of a dissident minority, even by his own party. In the same period, Roy Hattersley moved from being the Labour Party's Deputy Leader to one of its most outspoken critics. These two examples indicate the way in which politics itself alters the interplay between political ideas, political actors and ideological traditions.

We also need to distinguish between different levels of dissent. Some of the examples above are often seen as anti-systemic forms of dissent, that is dissent which seeks to challenge the structural basis of society, or to defy totalitarian systems or monolithic ideologies. At this level it would also include Marxist revolutionaries who do not accept the economic rationale of capitalist societies and who attempt to replace it with an alternative socio-economic order. Or it would include dissidents seeking to overthrow dictatorships. Dissent also works at other levels, confined within existing systems, that may take the form of defying a particular law or policy or in members of a political party refusing to go along with the positions of their leaders. In these cases, dissent is often linked to a single issue which has aroused particular defiance. On the other hand, dissent also includes groups seeking 'exit' from mainstream society. These groups might include travellers or anarchists living in communes who do not seek to transform or overthrow the political system, or indeed even to establish a 'voice' within it. Rather they seek escape from its values and constraints and attempt to establish alternative ways of living.

This should help us to distinguish clearly between dissent and opposition. Dissent amounts to, in Scruton's words, a 'withholding of assent', that is a refusal to comply with laws, state policy or dominant ideological beliefs (Scruton, 1982, p.131). Opposition, on the other hand, is limited to the assertion or mobilization of an alternative political position. In addition to different dimensions of dissent, we also need to be aware that there are very different ways of dissenting as well as very different types of dissidents. One type of dissident is the public intellectual who, by definition, assumes the role of disseminating ideas and influencing public debates. Such intellectuals are often regarded as typical dissidents because of their ability, through writing, to raise difficult questions without being obliged to defend partisan political positions. In this way intellectuals are often distinguished by their priority of pursuing 'truth' rather than accepting received wisdom. Their role as dissidents is often that of mediators of heretical positions, in which they 'go against the grain' of mainstream public opinion. This might explain why intellectuals are often regarded as awkward, troublesome, unreliable or disloyal. Yet, many would argue that without this role of independent thinking and commitment to non-partisan intellectual inquiry, orthodoxies would never be challenged and the opportunities for political change would be severely limited. It is noticeable that the challenge to totalitarian regimes often attracts notice through the activities of intellectuals, be they writers, artists or film directors whose work is often banned or severely restricted, when it is seen as threatening to the state.

In his study of right-wing think tanks, Richard Cockett (1994) found that intellectuals were crucial in the mediation and consolidation of new ideas which helped develop the neo-liberal agendas of the Thatcher governments in the 1980s and 1990s, as they attempted to construct an alternative to the post-Second World War consensus; one which had been dominated by Keynesian economics and social democratic welfare reform. One important figure here is F.A. Hayek, the Austrian economist and theorist whose works were the most influential on the ideology of these governments. His own rise to prominence provides an illuminating example of how public intellectuals can influence debate. It shows how dissent, as the basis of the mediation between intellectuals and public life, can shape or reinvent politics. Hayek's early major work, *The Road to Serfdom*, was published in 1944 at the beginning of the golden era of social democracy and the expansion of the welfare states in Western Europe. As such it was regarded as heretical; it was, if you like, on 'the margins' of political debate. For many critics his views were out of date and failed to engage with the modernizing direction of Western societies. At the time it was a book that attracted limited interest. Yet in the 1980s Hayek became a 'mainstream' thinker. In the very different political climate of high unemployment and following more than 30 years of the welfare state, his views were taken up by governments in Europe and the USA. His arguments had not changed significantly; yet he was now regarded as a 'guru'. Students even began to read *The Road to Serfdom*!

Social movements can provide other examples of political dissent, though a social movement may be merely oppositional rather than dissident. Since the 1960s in particular a whole range of dissident social movements have emerged for a variety of different reasons. One reason was a reaction to the materialism of consumer capitalism, by movements such as the hippies, who sought to 'drop out' from the values of mainstream society, or attempted to create a counter culture. Others included feminists on 'reclaim the streets' marches, while students throughout Europe challenged the elitism of higher education. Other dissident movements, notably in the USA, fought civil rights struggles for racial equality. More recent examples would include anti-roads protesters and pro-hunting groups. One reason often cited for the rise of many social movements has been the attraction of their dissident stance in contrast to political parties that (so it is argued) have become overly integrated into the mainstream. Movements often focus on a single issue of perceived injustice, while parties include whole packages of beliefs and political traditions. In the same way that not all intellectuals are dissidents, not all movements can be described in this way.

A further question worth posing here is whether dissent can take violent forms. Is terrorism a form of dissent for example? There is no easy answer to this. Many political theorists and writers would add the qualification of 'legitimate' or 'illegitimate' dissent. That is dissent expressed in liberal democratic societies is only legitimate if it does not resort to violence. Yet this seems to take us only part of the way. For example, deciding what is legitimate or illegitimate dissent will depend to some extent on ideological assumptions, cultural influences and political tradition. Meanings can also change over time, suggesting that one person's freedom fighter is another person's terrorist. This was the case with the African National Congress (ANC) for example, described by many opponents (including the Thatcher governments in the UK in the 1980s) as 'terrorist' because of its commitment to armed struggle. Yet following the release of Nelson Mandela in 1989 and the participation in the new post-apartheid South African government in the 1990s, this description was changed and the ANC became regarded as a mainstream political organization. This suggests a further point of demarcation between forms of dissent based on commitment to democratic values and different types of dissent, including violent ones which may assume a legitimacy in non-democratic societies on a 'last resort' principle.

We also need to be aware that interpretations of dissent are often restricted to a liberal democratic context. What about cases where democracy only partially exists, or democratic societies where minority groups perceive themselves as excluded and use violence as a 'last resort' in registering their dissent? The Weathermen, a group which grew out of the mainstream student movement in the USA in the late 1960s, ended up in the mid 1970s as a clandestine organization committed to occasional bombings of non-civilian targets in protest at the 'illegitimacy' of the US government in fighting the Vietnam War. The same period in Italy, known as 'the years of lead', included acts of violence carried out by 'right-wing' neo-fascist groups as well as left-wing terrorist groups such as the Red Brigades against what they saw as the collusion between the military and the Italian government. In the USA in the 1990s there was a spread of right-wing terrorist groups, often fuelled by fundamentalist Christian values, in opposition to abortion and homosexuality. More recently 'anti-globalization' demonstrators have questioned the legitimacy of the 'G8' countries to make decisions which have major implications for less developed countries' economies, while Islamic and Palestinian groups have taken violent actions in protest against what they see as the 'illegitimate' Israeli occupation of Palestine and the US invasion of Iraq.

We could also take the examples of many nationalist groups, such as those described by Saward in Chapter 2, who do not perceive their interests as being represented by the existing constitutional arrangements and engage in violent actions to bring attention to their plight. To decide whether an act merits the label of dissent, or whether a group or individual should be described as dissident, is not to endorse the particular cause. Rather the task of the political theorist and student of politics is to try and find an analytical framework which takes into account the multiple definitions and classifications of dissent.

FIGURE 3.2   Palestinian women protest about Israel's security barrier near Ramallah, July 2004

SUMMARY

- Dissent is crucial to politics, both as a political concept and as a living idea.

- Different dimensions of dissent can be classified according to whether they challenge the legitimacy of the state (and its laws) or challenge dominant beliefs and values.

- Dissent can take violent or non-violent forms and can be distinguished as 'legitimate' or 'illegitimate'.

- Dissent is different from opposition.

3 DISSENT AS A SET OF LIVING IDEAS

To describe dissent as a living idea or, perhaps more accurately as embodying a set of living ideas, is to say that historically it has had a role in influencing the direction of politics. The act of dissenting has brought together intellectuals, movements, social classes and political groups. In this way dissent, through the critique of injustice, the refusal to comply with laws or the need to challenge orthodox and dominant assumptions, has historically often been the trigger for social and political change.

As a way of illustrating the link between ideas, movements, intellectuals and dissent, politics in Britain in the late eighteenth century provides a rich example. This was a period described by the historian Roy Porter as the 'British Enlightenment', while it also included notable events further afield, including the American Revolution of 1776 and the French Revolution of 1789. The latter was inspired by the dissemination of dissident ideas during the French and European Enlightenment, a movement which involved the spreading of pamphlets and books, notably the *Encyclopeadie*, which included the writings of the '*philosophes*' such as Diderot, Voltaire and Rousseau, and stimulated much public discussion. A study of the Enlightenment and its legacy provides a classic example of how dissident ideas, that is ones first expressed from the 'margins', can become 'mainstream', to the extent that they are now seen as representing a new mode of thought, even a 'project', such was the extent of the Enlightenment's departure from existing ways of thinking about the world. The emphasis on science, reason, progress and secularism led to the birth of Western social science in subsequent years. It also helped to 'reinvent' politics, notably through the French Revolution, and provided new economic theories. These ideas were initially held by heretics, intent on disputing religious and other orthodoxies. Initially, the thinkers often met in small, sometimes clandestine, environments, in order to disseminate their ideas. Subsequently they were greatly helped by the expansion of communications, including the publication of journals and newspapers and cultural and educational initiatives such as libraries, musical events and art forms. There were no formal political parties or movements which would now be the most likely spaces for such public discussions. As well as public meetings, the ideas of the Enlightenment were also discussed in 'private' salons, often organized by women. The spreading of ideas in this way reminds us that the social and political context is important in understanding the formation and practice of dissent, processes which are often uneven and paradoxical. On the one hand, the salons allowed women the chance to share the ideas of the Enlightenment through discussions of the great issues of the day in their living rooms. On the other hand, the salons reflected inequalities of power between men and women. The speakers at the salons were usually men, with the women acting as hostesses. Not only were the women only partial citizens at this time, they could not even become full dissidents.

From the writings of the Enlightenment thinkers, we can discern the first modern (almost entirely male) 'public intellectuals', who began to replace the clergy as the sources of intellectual authority. The French term *philosophes* attached to the likes of Diderot and Voltaire, carries a more specific meaning as 'a man of letters who is also a freethinker'. As such they were 'cosmopolitans, citizens of an enlightened intellectual world who valued the interest of mankind above that of country or clan' (Hamilton, 1992, pp.24–5). The arrival of public intellectuals carries a particular implication for an understanding of the development of dissent. Unlike the clergy whose authority was rooted in religious, superstitious explanations and mainly protective of the existing social order, the *philosophes* had a completely different way of looking at the world. Their view that society could be understood and organized differently on the basis of knowledge, science and intellectual inquiry, was the governing claim of the Enlightenment. It was also very dangerous to the prevailing social order. To be a dissident, to dissent, was to move away from the authority of the church and traditional social hierarchies and put scientific methods and secular, 'humanist' thinking above religious or partisan allegiance. For Immanuel Kant, this emphasis on the pursuit of truth afforded by the Enlightenment meant man's escape from 'immaturity'. The freedom to think was crucial to the attainment of individual enlightenment. Kant (1983, p.41) urged people to 'dare to know' and 'have courage to use your own understanding'. Dissent, in his view, was as much a matter of private judgement as delivering a public lecture.

The 'British Enlightenment', a more modest affair, nevertheless contributed through its new ideas to wider processes of major social, economic and cultural change, and a particularly significant turning point in the development of modern politics in the UK. Some background to this political moment is necessary. The so-called 'Glorious Revolution' of 1688 promised parliamentary sovereignty, based on a separation of powers between monarchy and parliament, the rule of law and religious toleration. Indeed John Locke's *Two Treatises of Government*, written before the Glorious Revolution (though published in its aftermath), seemed to provide the classic statement of an emerging liberal order, one which would include religious toleration and even the right of dissent, in the form of rebellion, if governments reneged on their 'contract' with the people.

According to Roy Porter there was 'exceptional freedom of expression' from this time in which the 'constitutional and ecclesiastical framework seemed to guarantee fundamental freedoms' (Porter, 2000, p.34). By the mid eighteenth century, alongside major industrial, economic and scientific change, there was also an explosion of ideas and the rapid emergence of new cultural forms, as well as the development of public life, such as museums, art galleries and the post office. The dissemination of political ideas and debate was arguably the most vivid example of this emerging civic culture. Coffee houses, to Porter, 'the seats of English liberty', were a particular source of ideas, providing unofficial 'seminars for news, novelty and gossip'. He claims that by 1739 there were 551 coffee houses in London alone. Here, newspapers and pamphlets were provided and 'critics held forth and debates raged on the latest opera, political squib, court scandal or heretical sermon' (Porter, 2000, pp.35–6). This expansion of civic life, fostered by a less censorious climate, could therefore be seen as increasing the opportunities for dissent.

Yet there was an imbalance between these new spheres of dissent and the political system. Many felt that the 1688 reforms had not gone far enough and that a combination of 'aristocratic capitalism' (in Porter's words) and a coercive state, in which church hierarchies were dominant, had prevented major change. One source of dissent took a religious form with significant public and civic implications. A group which came to be known as the Rational Dissenters had refused to subscribe to the articles and principles of the Anglican church, thereby risking exclusion from public life, and set up their own educational institutions, which became known as the 'dissenting academies'. These were built on the new freedom of thought, and in places such as Gloucester, Hinckley, Warrington and Kibworth academies, non-conformist ideas were encouraged, as a challenge to traditional schools and universities. As a result, known Rational Dissenters were banned from public life, their ideas regarded as subversive by those in power. Their teaching methods were liberal and the curriculum, with the work of Locke prominent on the recommended reading list, emphasized free inquiry and the furtherance of liberty. In the politics of the time, these academies of dissent became a significant political force in the mid to late eighteenth century, a period of major political turmoil in Europe. In an age when political parties were still to be formed, they provided important spaces for the dissemination of ideas.

One of the earliest academies, Hoxton in east London, was a formative influence on William Godwin, who was to become a leading dissident and anarchist. Godwin, son of a dissenting minister, was one of 30 boarders at the academy and attributed his subsequent dissident outlook to his educational upbringing:

> 'Why should I?', such was the language of my solitary meditations, 'because I was born in a certain degree of latitude, in a certain century, in a country where certain institutions prevail and of parents protesting a certain faith, take it for granted that all is right'?
>
> (Godwin, 1993a, pp.218–19; first published 1831)

What Godwin took from the Rational Dissenters was the right to freely exercise private judgement and the belief that this would lead to the furtherance of truth and progress. Like Kant, he believed enlightenment to be the culmination of individual maturity. Dissent, in the first instance, was to be found in the capacity of individuals to use their reason in making critical judgements. His views, also heavily influenced by the French Enlightenment, were set out in his major political work, *An Enquiry Concerning Political Justice* (1793). Here, in one of the first anarchist expositions, Godwin argued that the state itself was a 'disenlightening force', by virtue of its preference for coercion over reason and freedom. For him 'reason is the only legislator' (Godwin, 1993b, p.95). Power, law and punishment had no legitimacy because they were founded on coercive and therefore irrational principles. Moreover, in contrast to social contract theorists such as Locke and Hobbes, he questioned the authority of the state, rejecting the view that individuals had consented to obey its laws as a precondition for securing their freedoms. For Godwin, society, driven by the increasing surge towards reason, would have no need for such a body; individuals left to their private conscience would exist peacefully in a community of parishes.

Although his views in *An Enquiry Concerning Political Justice* were heretical by any standard, they were not deemed sufficiently threatening to prevent publication, according to William Pitt the prime minister, on the grounds that its price would put it out of the reach of most ordinary people. This was not the case, however, for others in the radical circle of intellectuals to which Godwin belonged. These included the civic republican, Thomas Paine, Mary Wollstonecraft an early feminist (whom Godwin later married), the publisher Joseph Johnson, and the artist–poet William Blake. Following the French Revolution of 1789, the political climate in Britain changed and the role of dissidents became more significant and, for the state, threatening, as arguments in favour of the revolution were heard. In a famous sermon in Britain four months after the French events, the Reverend Richard Price, a dissenting minister, delivered a warning to the existing rulers, that they must choose between 'darkness' and 'light'; in effect either defend the old order, or recognize what he thought to be the inevitable move towards liberty and progress which the French Revolution represented.

His sermon provided the stimulus for several developments. First, Edmund Burke published a critique of the French Revolution, *Reflections on the Revolution in France* (1791), which was also a defence of the existing British political system and now seen as the founding statement of modern conservative principles. Burke (1982) argued against the French Revolution on the grounds that it had been driven by abstract theories of reason with no grounding of experience and would lead to conflict and instability and, moreover, was particularly inappropriate for British conditions which had benefited from gradual evolution.

Next, Thomas Paine responded to Burke by endorsing the principles of the revolution and arguing that Britain needed a similar constitutional upheaval.

FIGURE 3.3 William Godwin

For Paine, who had earlier been a prominent advocate of the American Revolution of 1776, Britain was an *ancien régime* which, because it was dominated by an aristocratic political elite, preferred the values of deference over equality, tradition and prejudice over reason and monarchy over democracy, needed similar revolutionary change. In *The Rights of Man* (1791), Paine argued that all individuals are born with inalienable rights, to liberty, property and security, and that the purpose of the state is to defend and uphold these rights. However, in order for this to happen, these principles needed to be incorporated in a constitution to be drawn up by a constitutional convention, involving representatives of the people. According to Paine this meant that the existing British system, despite the reforms of 1688, continued to be maintained by aristocracy and hereditary privilege.

The publication of *The Rights of Man* had major political repercussions. It sold over 40,000 copies in a matter of months. Paine himself, however, had to flee the country after charges of sedition were made against him and in 1792 he was found guilty *in absentia* of seditious libel and outlawed from returning to Britain (he had fled to France). In addition the booksellers who sold the publication were imprisoned. However, there were wider implications which illustrate the impact dissent can have on politics. A range of dissident movements which advocated the 'rights of man', the ideals of the French Revolution and free speech were now involved in major demonstrations and protests in London. These included the London Revolution Society, the London Corresponding Society and the Society for Constitutional Information. In its now stringent efforts to eradicate dissent, a series of Treason Trials was held between 1793 and 1795, while the two so-called 'Gagging Acts', the Seditious Meetings Act and the Treasonable Practices Act, which parliament had passed, outlawed 'seditious meetings', those public meetings deemed to incite opposition to the state, and seditious writings, those deemed treasonable.

Although Mary Wollstonecraft was part of the same circle and a fellow admirer of the French Revolution, her status as a leading dissident at the time has a different dimension. She too was driven by the belief, shared by Paine and Godwin, that reason would be the guide to a more egalitarian and just social order. She anticipated Paine's arguments for natural and civil rights, in *A Vindication of the Rights of Men* (1790), but raised a whole set of new ideas in *A Vindication of the Rights of Woman* (1792). One of the earliest statements of feminism and written in six weeks, Wollstonecraft addressed the political subordination of women. She argued that though women had the same natural rights as men, society was ordered in such a way that they were denied full citizenship. Moreover this denial of citizenship was sustained not only by a lack of legal rights to equal education and property ownership, but through the dominant value system. Women, encouraged to be submissive and passive, were effectively 'socialized' (to use a more recent term) into specific roles. Therefore 'enlightenment' and 'reason' had a particular, different, implication for women. In order to be full 'active citizens', a 'revolution in female manners' (or gender roles) was needed (Wollstonecraft,

1975, p.132). According to Wollstonecraft, women should be treated as 'rational creatures, instead of flattering their fascinating graces and viewing them as if they were in a state of perpetual childhood, unable to stand alone' (Wollstonecraft, 1975, p.81). What Wollstonecraft was proposing, therefore, was a transformation in the role of women, a transformation that would extend to the political system as a whole. Women, she said, 'must only bow to the authority of reason, instead of being the modest slaves of opinion' (Wollstonecraft, 1975, p.139).

The example of the British Enlightenment dissidents, outlined above, provides us with some insight into the way in which dissent 'works' as a set of living ideas in a particular political context. First, it is evident that there were many different ways or methods of expressing dissent. These included the writing of articles, books and pamphlets, Reverend Price's sermon, mass protests and, through the academies of dissent, alternative educational institutions. Dissidents included intellectuals, who spoke out in books, pamphlets and in public discussions, in favour of civil rights, political change and social movements which took to the street to protest.

FIGURE 3.4 Mary Wollstonecraft

Second, the different dimensions of dissent were apparent. Godwin's critique of the legitimacy of the state was one example of the first dimension; another was Paine's critique of the lack of rights, democracy and the existing constitutional framework; the protests in the mid 1790s also challenged the lack of democracy and citizenship and contested the authority of the state. Also evident was the second dimension of dissent: the objection to dominant beliefs in helping to legitimize imbalances of power and social inequalities. Wollstonecraft's objection to the pervasiveness of submissive and patriarchal ideas and her call for a 'revolution in female manners', is a clear example of that, while the dissenting academies provided a challenge to the norms and values that mainstream establishments were promoting. 'While your universities resemble pools of stagnant water', Joseph Priestley the Rational Dissenter wrote to William Pitt the prime minister in an open letter, 'ours are like rivers, which taking their natural course, fertilize a whole country' (in Porter, 2000, p.406). Godwin and Wollstonecraft themselves started separate schools along similar lines with limited success. The Enlightenment itself represented to some extent a stream of dissident ideas, reason and progress, secularism and natural rights. Dissent in this context, according to Roy Porter, was 'the spear to truth' (Porter, 2000, p.xxi). It had a crucial role in influencing political change. It did this by redrawing political boundaries, and in providing new ideas and arguments was crucial in the 'reinvention of politics' at this time.

The response of the state to the dissidents illustrates the challenge which political dissent can make on power. During the 1790s different forms of responses are evident. The 'Gagging Acts' were the most repressive acts of state legislation, aimed at preventing dissent, whether in speeches or publications (in the case of *The Rights of Man*). Wollstonecraft was demonized as 'a hyena in petticoats', while Paine was a 'traitor', and Godwin's ideas were the subject of satire in many popular comics. Populist backlash, in the form of street battles and heckling and seeking out dissidents, also took place in some cities and was a further way of denouncing dissent and reaffirming the existing political order. This demonization of dissent indicates the dangers and risks afforded by dissidents, while illustrating the measures those in political authority may be prepared to take in order to stop them. Moreover, what made the dissidents of the 1790s so dangerous for the political authorities was that their ideas set out in books and pamphlets had a wider and immediate public appeal. As 'living ideas', which mingled with the activities of political activists and thinkers, they came 'alive' in a specific historical period to influence arguments for political and social change, ones seen as revolutionary at the time.

SUMMARY

- Public intellectuals, from the Enlightenment onwards, have had an important role in disseminating heretical ideas and influencing political debates.
- In Britain new spaces for dissent were created by the expansion of public life from the eighteenth century.
- The ideas of 'British Enlightenment' dissidents such as Godwin, Paine and Wollstonecraft have had an important impact on the development of modern political thought.
- The response of the state to the 'British Enlightenment' dissidents (for example the attempt to prosecute Paine and the demonization of Wollstonecraft), reflects the dangers and risks many dissidents face when they set out their views.

4 POLITICAL THEORY AND DISSENT

The discussion in the previous section focused on the ways in which ideas of dissent were articulated in a particular historical context and some of the impacts that they had – both for the lives of the dissidents, but also crucially for the bigger picture; namely the effect they had on the political rulers at a rapidly changing and critical time in British politics. Therefore, from this example, we can say that dissent was a type of political participation which questioned the 'legitimacy' of the political system, its institutions, laws and policies, but also its dominant values. It was pivotal to the reinvention of British political ideas in the late eighteenth century, a period many have identified in broader terms, following the French Revolution of 1789, with the formation of modern political ideologies. The terms 'left' and 'right', initially attributed to the seating arrangements which divided the groups in the new French parliament, became identified from this point on with ideas of progress, equality and social justice on the one hand, and order, tradition and social hierarchy on the other.

It is important to recognize how, in this case, dissent worked as a set of living ideas. The writings of intellectuals, the language of a popular pamphlet, the force of sermons and the discussions in the coffee houses helped produce a critique of the way politics was conducted and power was distributed. In this respect the impact of dissent as a set of living ideas is clear. In the case of Paine in particular, his pamphlet was widely read and the state responded by attempting to prosecute him. There is no doubt though that intellectuals had a role in mediating ideas to broader movements, if we look at the ideas of the Rational Dissenters for example, while they found a range of new outlets for the consumption of their publications.

However, there is a second way in which dissent worked as a set of living ideas at this time. The ideas of thinkers such as Godwin, Paine and Wollstonecraft were also to become part of a wider chain of ideas, that developed into political ideologies. Thus, Godwin's critique of the authority of the state, and his ultimate preference for a stateless society of parishes, was influential in the formation of the anarchist tradition of political thought. Mary Wollstonecraft's critique of what she called 'female manners' – now called 'patriarchy' – has been instrumental in the development of a feminist tradition of political thought, in particular liberal or first-wave feminism, which emphasized equal rights and opportunities for individuals, though arguably the strength of her critique of the values which underpinned the subordination of women would also link her to the more 'ideological' second-wave feminism of the 1960s and 1970s.

Paine's belief in the need to found a state upon citizen rights with a written constitution, put him in the liberal camp, albeit a particular strand of liberalism that is often called civic republicanism. The main ideas which characterize this approach are the belief in the need for a strong constitutional framework, citizen rights and 'popular sovereignty', ideas which are still fundamental to modern liberal democratic parties and movements. Though Paine had to leave the country and arguably had more influence in the USA than the UK in the eighteenth century, his ideas lived on, influencing the Chartists in the 1840s, a mainly working-class movement seeking universal suffrage and annual parliaments. Paine's ideas were given a more recent renaissance in the late 1980s when the pressure group Charter 88 was formed, calling for a written constitution, Bill of Rights, freedom of information and devolution. This emphasis on constitutional reform stimulated a new interest in Paine's work, and a serious attempt to reapply his ideas to the conditions of the late twentieth-century UK. This illustrates the way in which ideas which may appear long forgotten can once again return to the top of the political agenda and live on, in different circumstances. The 'latter-day Chartists' of the 1980s and 1990s had different ways of expressing their dissent, through petitions, vigils, letter writing, networking and conferences. They did not have to make the sacrifices of their predecessors, many of whom faced arrest or other penalties. Yet they were also dissidents, whose work had some influence on political power in the ideas which formed the New Labour governments from 1997, and which also influenced the political ideology of centre-left political parties and movements. This in turn started to put more emphasis on issues of justice and liberty.

Significantly, the outpouring of dissent in late eighteenth-century Britain had an effect on rival beliefs. Burke's response to Reverend Price's sermon – and more generally to the ideas which influenced the French Revolution – has been seen as the origins of modern conservative thought. In his response he is concerned about the destructive nature of dissent, the way in which the wisdom learned over long experience is rejected in favour of 'abstract' concepts of reason. This critique of the abstract and 'untried' theories and his belief that radical change goes against the 'consolidated wisdom' of the British constitution, learned over centuries, led him to the belief in the 'imperfection' of human behaviour.

In the contribution dissent made to the development of these ideologies two points are worth considering. First, ideologies contain a distinctive structure of meaning which is derived from their respective core concepts. After all, concepts such as freedom, justice and equality mean little on their own without some explanatory framework which suggests what kind of freedom, justice and equality is being demanded. In anarchist ideology, as expressed by Godwin and subsequently by other thinkers in this tradition, it is the state's illegitimacy that gave rise to dissent. For liberals, in the view of Paine and others, the absence of constitutional rights makes dissent important. In this way ideologies have a coherence in providing explanatory frameworks in order to explain political actions from particular standpoints and distinguish themselves from rival explanations. This only takes us so far, however. Ideologies often use the same political concepts, such as liberty, equality, justice or dissent. What becomes crucial, therefore, is the way in which these concepts are arranged. Michael Freeden describes this as the 'morphological approach to ideology'. His argument is that the meaning of an ideology is dependent upon the relationship between its different concepts. Using the example of justice, he argues that

[it] will possess a very different meaning if an ideology places it in close proximity to equality rather than to property. In the first case justice will always conjure up some form of equality – equality before the law, economic equality, gender equality and the like – while in the second it will always have to nod in the direction of property – protecting it through laws of inheritance or through banning invasive taxation.

(Freeden, 2003, pp.51–2)

If we applied the morphological approach to dissent we would also get different meanings depending on if it was placed next to equality or freedom, and these different meanings could be used, for example, by quite distinct left- and right-wing ideologies.

In the discussion above we saw how dissent as a living idea, mediated through intellectuals and political movements, connected with political ideologies. When we talk of liberalism, anarchism, feminism or conservatism, however, we are also talking about traditions of thought that have been used in a more relatively detached, analytical, way to make sense of political behaviour. This approach is central to what is called normative political theory, that is, broadly speaking, attempts to explain how a political system should be organized. In explaining how things 'ought to be', in this sense political theory also differs from a more 'descriptive' statement of how 'things are'. The object of political theory, according to Vincent (1997, p.254), is 'to make normative recommendations about matters of political concern'. It does this by taking a relatively detached standpoint in attempting to identify and explain the values, laws and norms of political behaviour. For Hindess, in the same collection of essays: 'Political theory suggests ... not only that societies are constituted on the basis of shared values (and penalties for their infringement) but also that these values and agreements are the principal means by which societies can and should be governed' (in Vincent, 1997, p.267).

If we apply the principles of political theory to dissent, what sort of judgements can we make about the place of dissent in modern politics? What would your views be, for example, on the legitimacy of the following examples of dissent?

1   A small group of demonstrators is prevented by the police from marching with banners calling for the execution of the Queen during golden jubilee celebrations in June 2002.

2   People refusing to pay the poll tax in the UK in the 1990s, which resulted in imprisonment in some cases.

3   During the period of apartheid in South Africa, many black people burned their pass books as a protest against racial segregation.

When thinking about your response to the above examples (all of which incidentally are true), it is worth considering the factors that might influence your argument. In other words, are there particular ideas that would influence your decision? You might have argued, for example, in relation to (1) that 'in a democracy, anyone should have the right to demonstrate about anything they wish', and therefore regard the decision of the police as 'unjust'. But could a similar approach be taken with (2), where in this case a law has been broken? And if so, are laws always to be obeyed or are there occasions where it is permissible to break the law? Think back to the discussion of civil disobedience in Section 1. Most people would argue that in the case of (3) a justified act of civil disobedience has taken place, against a state founded upon racism. These examples raise many questions, including the important point that ideas about dissent are contested; there is no single 'truth out there' to be found, though of course judgements can and will be made on the basis of what might be called our ideological preferences.

If, for example, we regard ourselves as liberals, the emphasis on equality before the law and freedom of expression would be paramount. If we see ourselves as conservatives then perhaps the need for social order and respect for tradition would lead us to agree with the restraints on the demonstrators in example (1). (In fact some liberals would also agree with this on the basis that there is a law on treason which the demonstrators could be said to be breaking.) In expressing a view about the above examples, many people would not think of themselves as following a particular 'tradition of thought'. This would suggest that ideologies have a more latent or hidden function; according to the Marxist thinker Louis Althusser (1984), ideologies 'interpellate' or 'hail' individuals, as a way of 'recruiting' them to particular positions. In other words, we are all influenced to some degree by ideologies even though we may not be aware of it. These ideologies resonate with our own experiences and provide a framework through which we make judgements, hold opinions and argue over political issues.

If we move to the world of the political theorist, we would need to stand back a bit and ask some deeper questions. The 'right to dissent', particularly in the first dimension as it has been outlined in this chapter, has been a much discussed theme in political theory. For Hobbes, writing shortly after the English Civil War of the 1640s, individuals, having consented to the authority of the state (or Leviathan), for reasons of individual security, to prevent anarchy and for society and culture to survive and prosper, had no right to dissent. In Locke's theory, on the other hand, individuals endowed with natural and civil rights before entry into the state had a different contract. The basis of the contract here was that individuals had an obligation to obey the state if the latter upheld individual rights, including property rights, and ultimately the 'right to resist' if the state failed to protect these rights.

In both cases 'consent' was also important, the extent to which individuals had 'consented' to obey the state. For Locke, individuals had only consented to obey the state if it upheld their freedoms; in the seventeenth and eighteenth centuries this was a radical notion (many would argue it still is) yet consistent with the rational reordering of politics, through modern constitutions. It also provided some of the key principles of liberal democratic theory, which merits more detailed discussion.

According to the liberal view, dissent is an important part of any free society and indeed, according to J.S. Mill, through the expression of rival and contrary views, is essential to the renewal of pluralism and democracy. In his view, regular political debate and discussion is essential to the pursuit and rediscovery of truth. Societies where dissent is prohibited are often described by liberals as 'totalitarian', 'authoritarian', or in other ways unfree. However, this only takes us so far. Clearly all forms of dissent for liberals are not permissible, while the right to dissent is also counter-balanced by other obligations. Bellamy sums up the liberal position well:

> We uphold the right of the political dissident to speak not because it is in his or her interests to do so, but because it is in the interests of all individuals living in a political society which depends for its openness and the free discussion and criticism of the policies and opinions of those in power. When the dissident's views appear to threaten the character of that society, then his or her right to express them becomes called in doubt.
>
> (Bellamy, 2000, p.146)

Therefore, according to this view, dissident views were crucial for ensuring liberty as well as for the development of democracy. We could say that they were also important in fomenting progress, by extending the realm of thought and criticism.

The remainder of this section will expand on these three liberal justifications for the rights of dissidents and provide evaluation from alternative theoretical positions, which have contested the underlying liberal view of freedom. First, the liberal emphasis on liberty as the core principle was on the basis that individuals should be left to their own choices. They know their own interests best, and it is not the business of the state (or any other 'collective' body) to interfere with freedom of thought or expression. The classic statement of this position can be found in John Stuart Mill's *On Liberty*. Writing in the mid nineteenth century, Mill was worried about the constraints of Victorian morality and culture. He was also concerned about the impact of a 'mass society' and the effects this was having on freedom of expression. According to Mill, the differing viewpoints and alternative opinions were getting lost; 'eccentricity', 'spontaneity', 'variety', 'diversity', were overridden by 'conformity' and 'public opinion'. At its worst it led to what he called the 'tyranny of public opinion'. Rather, Mill argued, individuals should be free to fulfil their own 'life plans', of 'tastes and pursuits', to 'suit our own character' (Mill, 1985, p.71).

Mill, like all liberals, did not believe that 'anything goes' as far as dissent was concerned. His attempts to provide the justification for the boundaries of dissent has been widely used as the liberal model. According to Mill, a distinction should be drawn between 'self-regarding' and 'other-regarding actions'. Self-regarding actions were those where the consequences of individual actions were confined to the individual himself/herself; other regarding actions were those where a consequence of an action could be said to affect others. In a famous passage he summarized the implications of applying this distinction in the following way; '... the only purpose for which power can be rightfully exercised over any member of a civilized community against his will, is to prevent harm to others' (Mill, 1985, p.68).

Mill used a further proviso, which was that a clear distinction should be made between liberty of opinions and liberty of action. The example he uses to explain this is the distinction between expressing the view that 'private property is robbery' and turning up at the house of a property owner (or 'corn dealer' to use his original example) to make this point. Mill also believed that dissident opinions had a wider benefit for the development of society. The 'peculiar evil of silencing the expression of an opinion is that it is robbing the human race of posterity as well as the existing generation – those who dissent from the opinion, still more than those who hold it' (Mill, 1985, p.76).

This view introduces the second liberal defence of dissent, which is that it was essential to progress. This position was apparent in Godwin's belief that the spirit of free enquiry would ultimately win out over ignorance and would be reflected in increasingly sophisticated and harmonious ways of living. In some ways Godwin represents the extreme interpretation of this position, by his belief in perfectibility; a more mainstream view from the *philosophes* of the French Enlightenment cemented the links between individual freedom, economic and social innovation and rational government, a position subsequently described as enlightenment rationalism: the belief that reason and the expansion of knowledge would provide modern societies with an increasingly 'progressive' turn. While this view was not peculiar to liberalism and had implications for a range of other theoretical standpoints such as Marxism and positivism, for liberals it was the stress on individual freedom that was the key to progress.

Third, liberals have justified dissent on democratic-pluralist grounds. In modern liberal democratic societies, where individuals are equal before the law, where voting and other political freedoms are recognized rights of citizenship, dissent is an essential part of the democratic process. This has its basis in the social contract theory of Locke, outlined above (though Locke was writing in pre-democratic times), where accountable government was the key element of a modern constitution. Traditionally, pluralists have argued that dissent is accommodated in a political system which allows the right to vote in regular elections, the right to join political parties or pressure groups autonomous from the state, an accountable legislature and equality before the law.

Attempts to evaluate the liberal view of dissent suggest some unresolved dilemmas in the liberal position which could be interpreted differently. Leaving aside problems of distinguishing between the boundaries of 'self' and 'other' regarding actions, some would also ask if the distinction was strong enough to resolve an apparent conflict between liberal and collective rights. How would you balance, for example, the rights of an organization which believes in racial hierarchies (say for example the British National Party) with those of a community with a high minority ethnic group composition? The case of the British writer Salman Rushdie in the 1980s who received a fatwa (in this case a sentence of death) by Islamic leaders over his book *The Satanic Verses*, provides a different angle on a similar problem. On the face of it, the liberal defence of his freedom of speech was clear. Yet, in theory, if his subject had been the Christian religion he could have been prosecuted for blasphemy, whereas Islam was not included in the blasphemy laws. Many liberals (perhaps following the tradition of the Rational Dissenters) would argue that there should not be any blasphemy laws in the first place. Additionally, questions were raised over the 'rights of a community', in this case those followers of Islam who may have been offended by Rushdie's arguments. In putting forward this position some critics argued that the 'Western' nature of liberalism meant it could not address the experiences and aspirations of other cultures.

A second criticism often made by the left – including Marxist critics – is that liberal theory underestimates power relationships in society, notably the economic interests of ruling groups. A range of examples could be used here. Universities, historically key institutions of free opinion and enquiry, have been subject to corporate and managerial pressures over the last 20 years, with implications for free speech and academic freedom, while they and other public sector institutions have seen rising prosecutions over 'whistle-blowing'. Other examples would include situations where the targets of dissent are major economic interests. The threat posed by anti-global capitalist protesters at meetings of the G7 and G8 from the late 1990s caused major constraints on demonstrations. At the G8 summit in Genoa in 2001, this included the cordoning off of the city centre and the imposition of zones denying rights of access to demonstrators. The USA, by virtue of its modern constitution regarded as the epitome of liberal free speech, has been a frequent subject of criticism for restricting dissent, for example in the 'McCarthyism' era during the Cold War in the 1950s, against the civil rights movements in the 1960s, and in the aftermath of the terrorist attack in September 2001.

Following Burke, conservative critics of liberalism have pointed to the destructive consequences of dissent. For conservatives a more important question is not the 'right to dissent' but the consequences for social cohesion, family life and the social order of those actions or beliefs. To some extent this comes from a more pessimistic view of human nature, notably a belief in 'imperfection' and the limits of what free individuals can achieve in harmony with social cohesion. The dissident movements of the 1960s, for example, were thought by many conservatives to be destructive and to have led to an imbalance between duties (or responsibilities) and rights, a view extended beyond the conservative tradition, to include 'communitarian' thinkers.

SUMMARY

- Political theory helps us to analyse what the limits and extent of dissent ought to be in any given political system.

- How we understand what the boundaries of dissent should be is influenced to an extent by our ideological preferences.

- Dissent occupies an important position in liberal theory because it provides the opportunity for free expression, pluralism and progress.

- Critics of liberal theories of dissent have argued variously that it underestimates economic power relations, reflects dominant Western cultural assumptions or can have a destructive effect on the civic order.

5 IDEOLOGY: THE VEHICLE OF DISSENT?

Through the example of dissent, this chapter has looked at the ways in which ideas have helped to reinvent politics. In the late eighteenth century in Britain it was dissidents who kept ideas alive through their various forms of political participation. Political theorists, from a more detached standpoint, incorporated and applied political ideas in order to provide normative judgements to explain political behaviour; in this case what the limits to dissent should be in a given political order. We also need to be aware that dissident ideas 'live' through the extent to which they help inform the development of constitutions, to make a case for citizenship or to put forward critiques from rival positions. We have seen that dissent is also crucial to the development of political ideologies. According to Michael Freeden, ideologies are 'vehicles of dissent', and as such are 'an indispensable resource for the intelligent conducting and reinventing of politics in its variegated forms' (Freeden, 2001, p.1). As vehicles of dissent they create a pluralist space for rival views of how the world should be organized, the best way of achieving social justice, equality and freedom. In the ensuing arguments and counter-arguments, the battles of ideas, political changes will occur, and political systems may be transformed, or adapt, or be overthrown. In this way, Freeden argues, ideologies help 'reinvent' politics by providing a framework of beliefs through which people help make sense of their political world, formulate critiques and mobilize opinion for political change.

Yet many have argued in recent years that ideologies have been in decline, that we are now faced with a political world, where technology holds the key to progress, where the ideological divisions between left and right are breaking down, and where the rationalist and onward march of progress associated with the Enlightenment has come to an end. Such 'end of ideology'

FIGURE 3.5   A Cuban dissident reads a statement in church in Havana, Cuba, after delivering more than 14,000 signatures requesting a referendum on political reform and free expression, October 2003

arguments are not new. Daniel Bell argued that in the 1950s and 1960s technological changes, Keynesian consensus on welfare reform and full employment had taken away the necessity for the polarization of ideas and social conflict (Bell, 1962).

More recent arguments, from a similar starting point, have pointed to the demise of traditional ideologies in the face of economic globalization and major global political and cultural changes. Postmodernists, for example, have argued that the latter part of the twentieth century saw the end of the 'grand narratives', namely liberalism, Marxism and the other modern political ideologies that were a product of 'Enlightenment rationalism'. In the view of many postmodernist writers, ideologies have been unable to address the more fragmented 'localized' and 'micro' politics which shape social identity, where (to use the feminist slogan) the 'personal is political', and identities are fluid and defined in multiple ways.

A quite different view, though also one which declared the end of the prevailing ideological age, was put forward by Francis Fukuyama. Writing in the period which saw the revolutions in Eastern Europe in 1989, he argued famously that with the imminent collapse of communism and the increasing shift towards liberal democratic systems, the era of great ideological struggles between opposing systems was over; effectively the West had won and the 'end of history', could be declared in the sense that there was only one type of political system – liberal democracy – that had a proven record, other ideological belief systems had failed or were unviable.

In the mid to late 1990s the 'third way', as conceived first in the USA and then in the UK, under the influence of the sociologist Anthony Giddens, also attempted to embody a political approach free from what it saw as the constraints of 'ideological politics'. First, it emphasized what it saw as a pragmatic rather than ideological approach, arguing that 'what matters is what works'; therefore ideology should no longer be the driving force of policy. Think-tanks became integrated more into the structures of policy making (in contrast to the role performed by the New Right think-tanks in the 1970s and 1980s). Second, it accepted that ideological convergence would be the new reality for the future. In this case it sought to take ideas from different ideological traditions. Perhaps most significantly it argued that 'market freedoms' and 'social justice' were no longer incompatible as the ideological traditions of both the left and right had claimed (Giddens, 1998).

It is possible to accept that major changes to ideological frameworks have taken place without denying the need for ideologies per se. Indeed, it could be argued that one of the main aspects that needs consideration in any study of ideologies is their capacity to break-up and re-form. Ideologies are not static philosophical statements; rather they are in the process of constant flux and renegotiation. As vehicles of dissent they provide the channels through which new ideas take shape and develop into political critiques. They also give voice to marginal or eclectic ideas, thereby helping to formulate political challenges to accepted norms or setting out alternative world views and ways of living. As vehicles of dissent, ideologies help ideas to 'live' in new forms. They can also help facilitate 'marginal' views into the mainstream, put new ideas onto the political agenda or encourage new ways of thinking. It is the nature of political ideologies to incorporate new beliefs, to adapt to political and social changes and to attempt to cohere them into a political narrative. Examples of new ideological configurations include the changes in the UK Conservative Party from the late 1970s, where the influence of neo-liberal ideas helped shape a new political agenda of privatization and individualism as well as offering a new appeal to different social groups.

What is also apparent in the new ideological politics is the way in which ideas are discussed and disseminated. In earlier sections of this chapter, the different methods and ways of spreading ideas were outlined and these ranged from discussions in coffee houses, pamphlets and books to theatres and even a sermon. To this we could now add the increasing use of technology. At the Genoa G8 summit in 2001 referred to above for example, the websites of groups of protesters, whose ideological allegiances ranged from environmentalism, anarchism, neo-Marxism, liberalism and Quakerism, took on a range of functions. First, they were a source of communication in providing information on where to meet and how to avoid the red and yellow zone restrictions set up by the police on instructions of the Italian government. Second, they provided a source of political identity in putting forward a set of beliefs, including interpretations of the 'right to resist' as well as critiques of neo-liberalism. Third, they provided a space for ideological views, in debating the extent and limits of dissent during the summit.

Subsequently, in the disputes about violence following the summit, they provided space for 'redress'. Essentially, these websites provided new sites of dissent and new ways of promoting, developing and contesting ideas.

Accepting the basis of Freeden's argument, that ideologies live on in new forms and that they will remain crucial to future politics, means that it is premature to talk of the end of ideology. He argues that 'Far from witnessing the end of ideology, a plethora of new ideologies have continued to emerge ... while older ideologies have been undergoing continuous processes of breaking up and re-grouping ...' (Freeden, 2001, p.6). He distinguishes between some of the more conventional 'grand, full' ideologies and the more recent 'thin, partial, eclectic ones'. He envisages a more fluid interplay of the ideologies of the future, where the 'implosion' of 'full' ideologies will mean greater crossing of traditional boundaries (Freeden, 2001, p.11).

The root of these changes in the scope of ideologies, namely global economic and cultural transformations, more fragmented and differentiated social structures, new sources of social identity and revolutions in technology and communications, also carries significant implications for dissent. We are already seeing what could be called the 'dispersal of dissent', with the nation-state less central in the formation of political movements and the centres of power shifting. Paradoxically globalization both 'homogenizes' forms of dissent, in the case of bringing together anti-global capitalist demonstrators, as well as decentring it, by focusing on 'local', particular, experiences. For political theorists this is likely to pose some old questions in new forms. The difficulties, for example, of 'policing' the web could have implications for states seeking to provide a framework for dissent, while the forms of dissent are likely to be broader than in the past. Dissidents, meanwhile, may find new constraints and opportunities in the new spheres in which they find themselves.

REFERENCES

Bell, D. (1962) *The End of Ideology*, New York, Collier Books.

Bellamy, R. (2000) *Rethinking Liberalism*, London, Pinter.

Burke, E. (1982) *Reflections on the Revolution in France* (ed. Conor Cruise O'Brien), Harmondsworth, Penguin.

Cockett, R. (1994) *Thinking the Unthinkable: Think-Tanks and the Economic Counter Revolution 1931–1983*, London, Harper Collins.

Freeden, M. (2003) *Ideology: a Very Short Introduction*, Oxford, Oxford University Press.

Freeden, M. (ed.) (2001) *Reassessing Political Ideologies: The Durability of Dissent*, London, Routledge.

Giddens, A. (1998) *The Third Way*, Cambridge, Polity Press.

Godwin, W. (1993a; first published 1831) *Thoughts on Man* in *The Political and Philosophical Writings of William Godwin Vol. 6* (ed. M. Philp), London, William Pickering.

Godwin, W. (1993b; first published 1793) *An Enquiry Concerning Political Justice* in *The Political and Philosophical Writings of William Godwin Vol. 3* (ed. M. Philp), London, William Pickering.

Hamilton, P. (1992) 'The Enlightenment and the birth of social science' in Hall, S. and Gieben, B. (eds) *Formations of Modernity*, Cambridge, Polity Press/The Open University.

Hayek, F.A. (2001) *The Road to Serfdom*, London, Routledge.

Kant, I. (1983) 'An answer to the question: what is enlightenment?' in *Perpetual Peace and Other Essays*, Indianapolis, Hackett Publishing.

Locke, J. (2004) *Two Treatises of Government and a Letter Concerning Toleration*, New Haven, Yale University Press.

Mill, J.S. (1985) *On Liberty*, London, Penguin.

Paine, T. (1998) *The Rights of Man, Common Sense and Other Political Writings*, Oxford, Oxford University Press.

Porter, R. (2000) *Enlightenment: Britain and the Creation of the Modern World*, Harmondsworth, Allen Lane, Penguin.

Scruton, R. (1982) *A Dictionary of Political Thought*, Basingstoke, Macmillan.

Vincent, A. (1997) *Political Theory: Tradition, Diversity and Ideology*, Cambridge, Cambridge University Press.

Wollstonecraft, M. (1975) *A Vindication of the Rights of Woman*, Harmondsworth, Penguin.

FURTHER READING

Freeden, M. (2003) *Ideology: a Very Short Introduction*, Oxford, Oxford University Press.

Freeden, M. (ed.) (2001) *Reassessing Political Ideologies: The Durability of Dissent*, London, Routledge.

Vincent, A. (1997) *Political Theory: Tradition, Diversity and Ideology*, Cambridge, Cambridge University Press.

Searching for justice

David Middleton

Contents

1   INTRODUCTION

'Justice' is a loaded term, and how to treat people justly is an area of great debate in political theory and ideology. Issues of fairness, freedom and equality are all entangled within conceptions of justice. Is it fair, or just, if people have unequal incomes due to different talents or efforts? Is it fair, or just, that some have more opportunities in life due to their class background? What about taxation? Taxing the rich more than the poor seems 'just' and 'fair' to most people (though one key political philosopher, Robert Nozick, would not agree! – see below), but *how much* more is a key question.

What of justice in the context of equality and difference? Inequalities of various sorts (incomes, class, gender, ethnicity) are a key focus of debates on social justice, as are their contested causes and potential remedies. To treat citizens justly, should the state treat us all the same, or differently according to our different characters or needs? Which equalities, and what differences, *matter* for justice?

In this chapter we will look at some of the most influential theories of justice of recent decades, and assess how important ideas of equality and difference have been in their formation.

Social justice is a living idea shaped by, and reformulated in the light of, particular political events. Politicians in particular are keen to claim that their policies, but not the other party's, are motivated by considerations of social justice. For example, the UK Prime Minister, Tony Blair, claimed in a November 2003 interview that the 'central belief of the Labour Party is social justice'. Like political obligation, national identity and dissent, discussed in other chapters in this volume, social justice is also a *contested* idea, the meaning of which has been challenged, reasserted and debated in light of rival interpretations. Other parties and movements, for example, would challenge the UK Labour Party's commitment to social justice. They might see this as merely rhetoric, used to keep traditional party supporters happy. Like most living political ideas, social justice can act as shorthand for a range of different purposes, for example a commitment to reduce Third World debt, or legalize gay and lesbian marriages. In this way, social justice 'lives' as an important resource which many groups – especially those which think of themselves as egalitarians (see Box 4.1) – will use in ideological debate.

> ### BOX 4.1   **Egalitarianism**
>
> Egalitarianism is an approach to politics and society which involves a strong belief in one form of equality or another. It is often associated with socialists, for whom the attainment of equality is the overriding aim. Egalitarians range from those who believe in absolute equality of outcome to those who support a more limited type of equality of opportunity. Egalitarianism could embrace those who seek fair taxation, as well as those who believe real equality depends on more fundamental social transformation.

To pin down the meaning of social justice with any precision is difficult, so it is not surprising that there is no agreed definition used by political theorists. These differences of interpretation will feature strongly in this chapter – you will encounter a number of possibilities – while the real resonance social justice has in our everyday lives will also be an important thread. Even those who claim social justice is a 'mirage', such as the right-wing liberal theorist Friedrich von Hayek (1976; first published 1944) have had to engage with the concept and formulate their own critiques of theories of social justice.

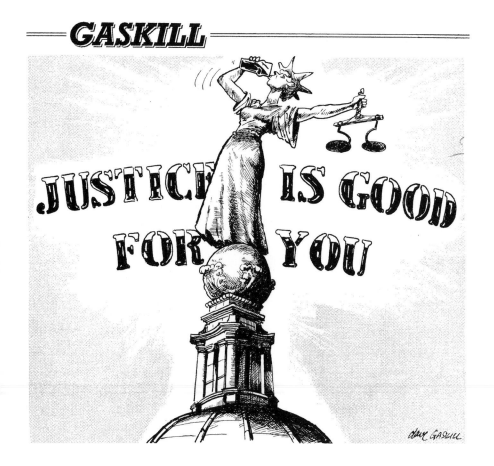

When we think of social justice as concerned with issues such as the distribution of wealth and income we can see the way in which political theory informs real world debates. Philosophers use the term 'essentially contested' to refer to concepts such as social justice which have been, and still are, the topic of hot debate both in political theory and in the world of practical politics. To put this simply, one's views on social justice are likely to be affected by one's views on politics more generally. Social justice is one part of a bigger 'world view'. A person with left-wing views, for example, is likely to take a distinctly different view of justice than one with right-wing views. To understand, therefore, the meaning of social justice it is necessary to recognize that different political perspectives approach the subject from distinctly different directions. Their disagreements help us to understand the ways in which political theory influences the debate on social justice.

SUMMARY

- Social justice is a contested political concept.
- Social justice is a living political idea with a long history.
- Debates about social justice are often debates about equality and difference.

2 THE SCOPE OF SOCIAL JUSTICE

Just think for a moment about the words that you would associate with social justice. What does the term mean to you? We have already mentioned fairness at the beginning of the chapter, but what other words would seem to you to have a connection to justice?

You might think that social justice has something to do with giving people their due, or perhaps you regard it as connected to impartiality, and therefore concerned with treating individuals in a way which is not discriminatory or prejudiced. You might think of justice as something connected to rights, and the idea that we are all entitled, as a matter of justice, to be treated in a certain way. But what does that way actually amount to? There are at least six ways in which we are accustomed to thinking about social justice.

To each the same amount;

To each according to their merits;

To each according to their efforts;

To each according to their needs;

To each according to their rank;

To each according to their legal entitlement.

(adapted from Perelman, 1963)

Let us think about what each of these might mean. The phrase '*to each the same amount*' implies that everybody would have exactly the same amount of some good or service, which Michael Walzer (1983) has called 'simple equality'. Suppose, for example, that you were at a party and asked to cut a cake so that every person in the party would receive a 'fair' share. What would you do? Most probably you would attempt to cut the cake into equal slices and then allow everybody else to pick first, leaving yourself the last piece of cake. In this way each person would receive more or less the same amount. But does the same principle apply, for example, to wages? Should the person who sweeps the floor receive the same wages as the engineer, for example? Even the idea of distributing a cake assumes that every person at the party has equal need of the same amount of cake. But the person closely watching their weight or the person with the large appetite are not equal in this respect. So whilst to *each the same thing* has a certain intuitive appeal as far as equality is concerned it is not effective in helping us to think about the important differences between people. It also takes no account of whether people are deserving of what they get, whether they need what they are given, or whether anybody else has a prior right to that which is being distributed.

The second conception, '*to each according to their merits*', could be expressed in the phrase 'getting their just deserts'. Strictly speaking desert and merit are not the same, but for the purposes of this discussion we will treat them as if they were. When distributing examination grades to students a fair procedure is to grade their work according to some pre-determined criteria and then those who fulfil those criteria deserve the best grades. Procedurally this seems fair and whilst it does not create an equal outcome, it does account for differences among people. But, is merit the best principle for distributing other goods?

Let us take the example of jobs. The application of what has become known as 'the merit principle' in shortlisting and hiring assumes that it is possible to measure a person's merit by their past behaviour, demonstrated by their qualifications and experience. But, as Young (1990) points out, whilst qualifications, experience and job-specific tests appear to be neutral, often they are culturally determined in a way which directly discriminates against specific groups: women, minority ethnic groups, disabled people, etc. Moreover, what counts as a merit is also difficult to quantify. Edwards (1995) has argued that although we are accustomed to thinking of merit in terms of qualifications, it might be possible to stretch the merit principle temporarily to include such things as 'race' and 'ethnicity' in order to give those groups denied access to the more prestigious jobs in the past an opportunity to acquire them now. The problem of 'merit' then seems to be that it is not as easy to define as many people might assume.

The third conception on Perelman's list, '*to each according to their efforts*', is closely related to merit in that it proposes that a person should get out of society what they put in. This would only produce an equal outcome if people contributed an equal amount. In reality, of course, this conception of justice favours those who work hardest and is concerned therefore to reward differences of effort. This is rather different from sharing the cake equally. Joseph and Sumption (1979) use a clever argument against the cake analogy when they say that although all might want an equal share, what if only one person made the cake? Do they not have a greater right to the cake for the extra effort that they put in?

Effort and talent play a significant role in social justice discourses, and it certainly seems fair to argue that those who put the most in should receive the most. However, as Young (1990) also points out, in complex societies it is often difficult to work out the relative input of each person. Therefore, designing a principle of justice based on 'what people bring to the table' is not only likely to be unfair, but also practically impossible to apply. Despite this, the idea that effort should be rewarded remains a popular one. Suppose, for example, that it was proposed that those students who worked hardest were to receive the highest grades? This might seem fair to the hard-working student, but what if all the hard work totally missed the point of the course? Arguably, when it comes to the distribution of grades, the student who does no work but fulfils all the criteria is more entitled to the high grade than the one who burns the midnight oil but is simply not as adept at fulfilling the criteria.

The fourth way of thinking about justice, '*to each according to their needs*', requires us to compare people's needs with their wants. Let us suppose that every person needs food, water and shelter. Societies, if they are to be stable and prosperous, must fulfil these 'basic needs' (Doyal and Gough, 1991). Any society that fails to meet these basic needs is likely to be judged to be unjust, but also is likely to face internal dissent from those denied access to goods others take for granted. The question is at what level of poverty, famine or homelessness do societies become untenable? Certainly, societies such as the modern UK seem able to exist with poverty and homelessness and there is not a continuous public outcry about the presence of these conditions.

FIGURE 4.1   Inequalities at a sports event in Burkina Faso

If society chose to distribute goods on the basis of need, then clearly this would mean some quite strong form of redistribution of wealth toward those who have the least. This would have to be done either directly (that is giving people the goods that they require or the means to acquire them) or indirectly (by funding projects with the responsibility to overcome poverty or homelessness). However, whilst most people have no strong objection to need as a principle of justice, they cannot agree so readily at what level need should be satisfied. Part of the problem here is that what people 'need' and what they 'want' are not necessarily the same thing. For example, an alcoholic probably wants more alcohol, but what they may really need is a strategy to help them stop drinking. In this example, the need and the want seem to be in direct competition with each other. Need is another principle that seems to prioritize difference. But often differences in need are socially created in the first place and can simply be the result of bad luck.

The fifth conception, '*to each according to their rank*', might seem an outdated way of thinking about justice. In a society in which all are nominally equal the idea that distribution should occur on the basis of rank, birthright or caste seems anachronistic. Nevertheless, political privilege is still distributed, to some extent, according to birthright (see **Mitchell, 2005**). Income is certainly distributed according to hierarchical structures. Managing directors receive more pay than shop floor workers. Whilst this might be because of merit or effort, it is also clearly affected by rank and social inequality. Certainly, Western liberal democracies like to think that rank has little significance these days, but some systematic and predictable effects are noticeable, such as women and minority ethnic groups receiving less pay, and accumulating less wealth on average than men or majority ethnic groups. This is true of most, if not all, countries of the world. So, whilst rank might not seem a prime suspect as a principle of justice in theory, in practice something close to rank continues to play an important role in the distribution of jobs, wealth and income.

Finally, Perelman suggests distribution on the basis of '*to each according to their legal entitlement*'. This means that you receive exactly that which is yours by legal right. This is a principle which is socially contingent as laws change over time. It could be used to promote either equality or difference depending on which is the dominant view of the law-makers.

There is one important point to note as we conclude this section of the chapter. In talking about 'social justice' we have been emphasizing 'distributive justice' – how much of a good, product, or benefit each person should receive, and the grounds for giving them what they receive. Whilst it is probably true to say that the majority of debate around social justice has been on questions of distribution, it is also true that the emphasis on the distribution of material or tangible goods excludes many other things which some think should be included in a theory of justice. Iris Young (1990), for example, argues that the emphasis on distribution of material goods leaves unaddressed questions of systemic oppression, such as sexism and racism, which are important for social justice. She notes that the primary emphasis of writers on social justice has been the distribution of wealth and income, and the distribution of occupational positions. David Miller (1976), for example, whilst supporting the emphasis on distributive justice, notes that this means that 'goods' such as self-respect are, at least, difficult to deal with – for in what way can we be said to distribute self-respect?

However, social justice has traditionally been conceptualized fairly narrowly as the distribution of material resources, and much of the argument about this has been concerned with how equal should people's access to resources be, and what grounds are there for inequality. Indeed, we could conceptualize this in terms of a debate between equality and difference. Questions of distribution are not simply about who gets what, but go to the heart of a debate about what people deserve to get.

SUMMARY

- There are many different interpretations of social justice.
- The weighting various 'distributive' principles are given differs from one society and context to another.
- We can think about social justice in terms of simple equality, merit, effort, need, rank and legal entitlement.
- The normal emphasis on distribution can lead us to overlook oppressive social processes along with intangible goods such as self-respect.

3 EQUALITY AND FAIRNESS AS PRINCIPLES OF JUSTICE

The idea of equality forms the basis of most modern theories of social justice. But the *concept* of equality allows for a range of different *conceptions* of equality, and these different conceptions are set out in a variety of different theories. The importance of equality to social justice should come as no surprise: equality seems an obvious solution to inequality. Certainly, equality has a powerful feel to it such that even those who oppose it must find special justification for doing so. Equality also features in one way or another in most modern political ideologies. As Michael Freeden (2003, p.72) notes: 'There is now a common acceptance of equality as a key concept, though not of its various conceptions.'

Equality, then, is a complex and contested concept, as well as being basic to different theories of social justice. The debates come in a variety of forms. For example, some people suggest that human nature itself is opposed to the idea of equality. The theme that the differences among people are so significant that they render equality impossible to achieve, is a constant one in the literature on social justice. Others argue that to concentrate on different talents and abilities is merely to aggrandize what are, to all intents and purposes, contingencies of luck. Such a view is associated with the most important political philosopher of recent times: John Rawls. The rest of this section will set out his influential, and much debated, theory of social justice.

Rawls's theory is a contemporary variant of a classic approach in political theory: social contract theory (see Chapter 1). He attacked his main liberal opponents, the utilitarians, for not taking rights seriously. Utilitarians seek to maximize overall utility or happiness in a society. According to Rawls, utilitarians would be happy with an overall increase in utility or happiness, even if its distribution was terribly uneven and many people could not share in it (or worse, were exploited to produce greater utility for others). He argued that: 'In a just society the rights secured by justice are not subject to political bargaining or to the calculus of social interests' (Rawls, 1971, p.4). The happiness of the few could not be sacrificed for an increase in happiness for the many. Governments and citizens were constrained by rights that must be respected even if ignoring them were beneficial in other ways. All citizens have these rights equally, they cannot be taken away from them. Or as the philosophers put it, the right has priority over the good. Treating people justly as individuals comes before maximizing happiness in the larger group or society.

At the core of Rawls's theory were the two principles of justice:

1   Each person is to have equal right to the most extensive liberty compatible with a similar liberty for others (Rawls, 1971, p.60).

2   Social and economic inequalities are to satisfy two conditions: first, they are to be attached to offices and positions open to all under conditions of fair equality of opportunity, and, second, they are to be to the greatest benefit of the least advantaged members of society (the difference principle) (Rawls, 2001, pp.42–3).

This looks complex, but it is really a means of stating what many people already think. The first principle holds that we should be as free as possible to set the course of our own lives. Rawls is, after all, a liberal, and as such he values individual people and their freedom to live their lives as they choose. For Rawls, there is no higher value than liberty. Note too that he refers specifically to an 'equal right to the most extensive liberty'. So this is one way in which the concept of equality plays a part within his theory.

FIGURE 4.2   John Rawls

Rawls's second principle is divided into two parts. The second part, known as the 'difference principle', has provoked a great deal of discussion and debate. The core idea of the difference principle is the need to make inequalities work to the benefit of the least advantaged (or the 'worst off'). Rawls's core idea is that social and economic inequalities are not wrong, or bad, in themselves. They only become indefensible when they don't operate to improve the position of the worst off (such as those on the lowest incomes). Rawls views society as a large-scale experiment in social cooperation. The luck and the talents of the better off – including their genetic talents, which are just a matter of chance and are not 'deserved' – *can* be used to improve their own wealth and position. If this were not allowed, if we were to take a more radical, levelling egalitarian approach, then, according to Rawls, individuals would have few incentives to innovate and to create wealth. But, he argued, this is only acceptable up to a point. As long as those in the worst-off positions are benefiting *as well*, then inequalities can be just. Rawls himself seems to support this view when he says that the 'natural distribution [of talents] is neither just nor unjust; nor is it unjust that men are born into society at some particular position. These are simply natural facts. What is just and unjust is the way that institutions deal with these facts' (Rawls, 1971, p.102). In other words, where we are born in society is 'decided by the outcome of the natural lottery, and the outcome is arbitrary from a moral perspective' (Rawls, 1971, p.74). The difference principle takes account of the need to offer redress to 'undeserved inequalities' (Rawls, 1971, p.100). What this means is that more resources should be given to 'those with fewer native assets and to those born into the less favourable social position' (Rawls, 1971, p.100).

Rawls suggests that whilst people are 'morally equal', inequalities are often the result of luck or a 'natural lottery' and therefore undeserved. Given a just society, according to Rawls, these 'accidents of birth' should be ameliorated by the way in which the basic structure is devised.

In this way, although Rawls is an egalitarian liberal philosopher, he does find that some inequalities of wealth are acceptable. Not to accept this, he argues, would make everybody worse off. The upshot of Rawls's 'difference principle', then, is that it is okay to tax the rich disproportionately, just as long as the proceeds are used to help the poor (or the 'worst off'). It is okay primarily because the rich do not deserve the talents that they use to get rich. Other people could just as easily have been born with those talents – it is a genetic lottery.

Having principles is fine, of course, but why should we accept *these* ones? Rawls was in no doubt that we all would and should accept them. The two principles do not just come out of the blue, however. Rawls argues that they would be chosen in an *original position* behind a *veil of ignorance*. The original position is more-or-less Rawls's version of the much older 'state of nature' of famous contract theorists such as Hobbes, Locke and Rousseau. Rawls updates the state of nature for the twentieth and twenty-first centuries. His original position is an imaginary place, an 'initial position', outside society, where a group of people meet, in order to define 'the fundamental terms of their association', or, how their society should be shaped and run. People in the original position are behind a veil of ignorance: they don't know their age, class, religion, or any other particular facts about themselves. They are choosing, self-interested people, but stripped down to their human essence. In this odd, hypothetical position, behind the veil, Rawls asks: what principles would they (you, me) choose to govern the basic structure of society?

The trick behind the original position and the veil of ignorance is that, because we are stripped of our particular identities, we are forced to choose for everyone (or, for anyone we *might* be). If you can imagine yourself not knowing any of the basic facts about yourself – sex, age, ethnicity, etc. – but having to answer the question 'what principles of justice do you think society should be run by?', you will understand the original position. Indeed, Rawls argues that this self-reflection and questioning is what the 'original position' is all about – it is in our heads, not a real place. It is what Rawls terms a thought experiment.

In the original position self-interest is made to work for the common good. By using the position and the veil, writes Rawls (1971, p.19), 'One excludes the knowledge of those contingencies which sets men at odds and allows them to be guided by their prejudices'. When we all think ourselves into Rawls's original position, we are in a sense putting to one side for the moment our particular selves and lives; we are stripped down to our essence, ignorant of the real texture of our situated and complex lives. According to Rawls, the circumstances of the choices we make about social justice when we are in the original position makes the choice of his two principles fair and impartial.

We can step into the original position anytime, simply by putting ourselves mentally into it. So, now's your chance. Imagine you are one of the people in the original position. You are asked to devise principles of justice for society. What principles do you think you would argue for – distribution based on need, on merit, or effort, or some other criterion? Rawls assumes that in the original position we would all prioritize freedom of speech, expression, worship, and so on equally for all (the first principle), but that we would also want to guard against our being destitute at the bottom of the social and economic heap. We would do this by making sure the rich can only get richer if the poor also benefit in the process (the difference principle).

That is the gist of Rawls's theory of justice. We can see that the theory takes some account of both equality and difference – equality in both of his principles, and difference especially in the second principle. The theory has generated so much debate that thousands of articles have been written, subjecting each element of the argument to close examination. But the big picture is this: in 1971, this was an unusually ambitious and influential attempt to get to the root of what justice means, and why we should accept a just society along these lines. Referring to Rawls's revival of the idea that 'a person has a dignity and worth that social structures should not be permitted to violate', philosopher Martha Nussbaum writes that:

Thirty years after publication of A *Theory of Justice*, with all the discussion of rights and pluralism that has ensued, it is easy to forget that a whole generation of our political and moral philosophers had virtually stopped talking about that idea, and about how it can guide a religiously and ethnically diverse society like our own.

(Nussbaum, 2001)

SUMMARY

- Most theories of justice are based on the principle of equality in some way.
- Equality can mean different things, such as equality of wealth, status or power.
- Rawls's A *Theory of Justice* offers a contemporary version of social contract theory.
- The 'original position' is a thought experiment designed to focus our thinking on the nature of the just society.
- From behind the 'veil of ignorance', according to Rawls, rational persons would argue for two principles of justice which are built on distinctive conceptions of liberty and equality, including the controversial 'difference principle'.

4 DIFFERENCE AND ENTITLEMENT THEORY

Part of the problem with Rawls's theory, according to his critics, is that he has decided in advance what a just society ought to be like, and then devised his principles with the aim of securing that end-state. Moreover, the original position is hypothetical and, as Ronald Dworkin (1977) has pointed out, this means that it has no force in law. Trade unionists are keen on saying, 'a paper contract is not worth the paper it is written on'. So too the hypothetical original position is criticized because it is no more than an elaborate thought experiment. Others have defended Rawls's theory, suggesting that we need devices like the original position to be able to think clearly about the fundamental issues of justice, freedom and equality that are involved.

Rawls has been the major figure in Anglo-American political theory in recent decades, and as such his work has been targeted by a range of critics. One prominent early critic from the political right was Robert Nozick, who argued in *Anarchy, State and Utopia* (1974) that the type of redistributive policies that would follow from Rawls's idea of justice would require a state that was too big and which would undermine people's rights. A just society can't simply be designed or imposed, in his view (often called a 'libertarian' perspective).

Rather, societies come into being through a haphazard historical process, as a result of millions of choices made by thousands or millions of people. Any attempt to impose a pre-determined, for example egalitarian, end-state on society can only be managed with massive state interference. Ideals such as egalitarianism try to do the impossible, according to Nozick – to treat as equals people who are in fact very different.

Nozick's 'entitlement theory' is an attempt to satisfy two conditions of justice. First, the idea put simply is that what is yours is yours, provided you have come by it legally, and therefore nobody – including the state! – has the right to take it from you without your consent. Second, every person is different and that difference is so fundamental to what we are that any attempt to devise a just society will suit only the minority who are its architects.

Nozick's account of justice prioritized 'legal entitlement' over need, or merit. One has a right to one's possessions and their disposal. The only just or legitimate state, in his view, is a minimal state to settle disputes and to offer basic protection. A Nozickian minimal state would look quite different to contemporary welfare states; it would employ far fewer people, and would do far fewer things. It would run a series of courts, and would most likely have a defence force, but there would be nothing like a National Health Service or an education ministry. According to Nozick, there is no moral reason why anybody should be compelled to give up what is rightfully theirs for the sake of others – even if others need help or support. So there is no legitimate role for the state, for example, taxing people's wealth or incomes in order to provide social security or access to health and education for others. Nozick is opposed to egalitarianism because he regards egalitarians as committed to taking illegitimately from the better-off to benefit the less well-off. This critique forms the basis of what he calls 'entitlement theory' – if you are entitled to your 'holdings' or possessions, then it is a violation of your rights if the state or anyone else tries to force you to do something with them without your consent.

Nozick is not a social contract theorist, but he is a state of nature theorist. He asks us to go back, imaginatively, to a state of nature, as Locke does (see Chapter 1), to investigate what would happen as a result of people's unconstrained choices in such a position. He does not necessarily imagine that such a state of nature ever existed – this is something of a thought experiment too. Nozick argues that in a state of nature people seek protection from a 'minimal' state, dedicated solely to the security, protection and defence of its members, but not to some larger vision of their 'welfare' or society's welfare. What is crucial is people's rights: the opening lines of Nozick's book are 'People have rights, and there is nothing anyone can do to violate them'. This is a way of saying people are different, in their tastes and their choices and their outlooks. Attempts to make them equal in the sense of making them contribute to a common form of life or set of choices will undermine their rights.

Nozick's theory rests on a key argument about people and their possessions. First, he argues that provided holdings (goods or things that you possess) are acquired justly (e.g. not stolen or obtained by fraud) it does not matter how much a particular person possesses. Second, the transfer of holdings is just if the person doing the transferring (selling, giving, or bequeathing) does so freely, and provided that their original acquisition was itself just. In essence, that is the argument. The distribution of goods we end up with – whether goods or wealth are evenly distributed or heavily concentrated in a few hands – is just if goods were justly acquired and transferred. It does not matter to Nozick whether the distribution is uneven, or heavily concentrated in a few hands; all that matters is that goods are acquired legally.

Interestingly, Nozick does write briefly about a third principle, rectification, in addition to acquisition and transfer. He suggests that, where large-scale misappropriation or theft has occurred, then rectification needs to take place. This could mean, for example, large-scale compensation for Australian aboriginal communities whose land was taken from their ancestors. But Nozick asks more questions than he answers about rectification; in many ways that is not surprising, since it might undermine the very points he is keen to make about individual rights and the minimal state. If there were a widescale need for rectification, then one would need a more-than-minimal state to do it, a state that would have the right to interfere with individuals' 'holdings'.

If we put rectification to one side, the sum total of holdings in a society is just, from Nozick's point of view, if all holdings in the society have been acquired and transferred justly. Nozick defends his theory of 'justice as entitlement' on the grounds that, unlike its rivals, it takes account of the way that holdings emerged, and does not have a structural end-state in mind to which distribution must be forced to fit. His principles, he argues, are historical rather than end-state principles. In his view, we should accept as just a distribution which emerges historically from all the individual free choices that are made. We should not accept the ideas of others, such as Rawls, who would have us interfere with the free play of historical choice in order to impose (from the libertarian point of view) some egalitarian or other pattern or end-state which *they* think is more just. As noted previously, what Nozick calls the 'nightwatchman state' is a minimal state that protects our rights, but does not interfere with our liberty to dispose of our possessions as we see fit. In Nozick's view, modern states are too large, bureaucratic and interfering.

Nozick argues for equality only in the sense that we have equal rights to our holdings. In this way, he would broadly agree with Rawls's first principle, which is about maximizing individuals' equal freedom. But he is anti-egalitarian when it comes to any form of state redistribution of resources or wealth from the better off to the worse off. In considering Nozick's account, you might ask yourself: do I owe anything to those who are worse off than I am? Am I prepared, for example, to pay taxes to ensure that health care is available when it is needed? Would I be better off simply buying what I need, such as health insurance, rather than giving money to the state? Part of the argument he uses to support this position is the many and varied differences between people. He objects to state interference because, in part, he sees it as an effort to force very different people to be equal in the sense of living according to the same codes. He is a libertarian, and libertarians prioritize individual freedom. Nozick states, perfectly plausibly, that people 'differ in temperament, interests, intellectual ability, aspirations, natural bent, spiritual quests, and the kind of life they wish to lead. They diverge in the values they have and have different weightings for the values they share' (Nozick, 1974, pp.309–10). Given these basic differences between people, Nozick concludes that there can be no single system that suits everybody. For Nozick, the fact that even egalitarian writers are forced to concede that no one social system suits everybody provides the fullest possible proof that there is no one correct account of justice. What is needed, therefore, is a social system that allows for 'many different and divergent communities in which people lead different kinds of lives under different institutions' (Nozick, 1974, p.312). This is a description of what Nozick describes as 'utopia'.

Whether a Nozickian society would really maximize individual freedom is another matter. We might wonder whether so-called negative liberty, or the lack of constraints on people's action from the state, would really mean much to many people when material inequalities are great, and many lack the resources to exercise their supposed freedom (the ideas of 'positive' and 'negative' liberty are discussed in some detail in Chapter 5).

Nozick's point of view is, first, that those who argue for more material equality are simply envious of those that have made more of their opportunities. Second, equality is ruled out as a system of distribution because people are essentially different. Utopia, then, for Nozick is based on a vision in which we can each choose the life we want to live and are free to enjoy our possessions and to move between different types of communities. If a person happens to lack material resources, it is not a problem unless it can be shown that this is a result of unjust acquisition and transfer. If people wish to give to charity that is their decision, but society as a whole has no responsibility for the needy, and more importantly, no right to take from the wealthy to rectify poverty.

Nozick tries to challenge our common assumptions about welfare and end-state theories. Health care, he says, is often thought to be connected to people's needs, and many feel that need should be the only principle for allocating access to health care. But, he says, why should we stop at health care, what of barbers? Should a barber only cut the hair of those who need it? Similarly, should gardeners only attend to needy lawns? The question for Nozick is why should doctors be placed under an obligation to society that is

not present for other occupations? In criticizing the British philosopher, Bernard Williams, who argues for the distribution of health care according to need, Nozick says:

> He ignores the question of where the things or actions to be allocated and distributed come from. Consequently, he does not consider whether they come already tied to people who have entitlements over them (surely the case for service activities, which are people's actions), people who therefore may decide for themselves to whom they will give the thing and on what grounds.
>
> (Nozick, 1974, pp.234–5)

This is a forceful argument, for few people want to be forced to do things they would not otherwise do. Nevertheless, the argument has been criticized because in ruling out any form of redistribution from the better-off to the worse-off, Nozick seems to rule out our having a sense of justice, a sense of right and wrong (Heller, 1987).

Nozick implies a view of human beings who can develop their assets independently of other people. But, it could be argued, doctors are not simply born, they are made. Societies make decisions to allocate resources to train medical personnel and it is, therefore, at least arguable that those who benefit from the investment that society makes should give something back to the society. Nozick could counter this by saying that society invests through taxation, which he is opposed to in all but a minimal sense. The problem with this view is that without taxation it is unlikely that there would be any doctors; the form of social cooperation which Nozick seems to oppose is the very basis of the society which he would presumably support. It is a dilemma which, arguably, he is not able to solve.

Nozick has a further objection to redistributive equality. It is, he says, connected to envy. Envy he describes as a situation where you prefer a person not to have something that you do not have, regardless of the fact that their having it makes no difference to you either way. Let us suppose that your neighbour has a new car and you have an old banger. Envy is the situation where you would prefer that they did not have the new car, whereas jealousy is where you want a new car also. Why, he says, should we care what others have? The answer, for Nozick, is that we evaluate ourselves (and thus construct our self-esteem) by comparing ourselves with others. The problem is not that people do not deserve their place in the social hierarchy, but precisely that they do. Self-esteem, according to Nozick, is raised by the knowledge that we are better than others. Given that we are all different there is no point in trying to equalize that which nature makes unequal. Hence, equality is ruled out both as impractical and as failing to recognize our differences. One problem, however, with this account is that it does tend to run counter to what we know about self-esteem. There is a huge social psychological literature on self-esteem, but we need only note that most psychologists seem to agree that it is made only partly by comparisons with others. Nevertheless, we can see how a concentration on differences can be used in an argument against equality.

<table>
<tr><td rowspan="3">S U M M A R Y</td><td>

● Nozick's 'entitlement theory' argues that justice is concerned with what you have, how you came by it, and what you may do with it.

● Nozick's main argument against strong distributive equality is that people are different and they have different talents, aspirations and values.

● According to Nozick, a minimal state is all that is needed to protect our basic freedoms.
</td></tr>
</table>

5 THE TENSION BETWEEN LIBERTY AND EQUALITY

Equality often conflicts with liberty as we have seen in discussions of the work of Rawls and Nozick, for example. We might think of liberty as a condition in which our differences can flourish and equality as a condition where our differences need to be subsumed to a greater good. But is that a fair presentation of the argument? Is it possible for someone who believes in liberty to be an egalitarian? Or, a libertarian who believes in equality?

Rawls, for example, considers himself to be an egalitarian, but let's remind ourselves that his first principle is one which states that everybody should have the maximum liberty compatible with the same liberty for everybody else. That is, everybody should have 'equal liberty' even if they are unequal in other ways. So fundamental is this principle to Rawls's way of thinking that it is given priority over the other principles, including equality (of opportunity). But equal liberty does not mean infinite liberty. In other words, Rawls, and in this he follows the nineteenth-century English political theorist John Stuart Mill, believed that we should have only as much liberty as was possible without compromising others' liberty. This means that whilst we may have the freedom to party, we do not have the freedom to party all night long next to our neighbours who have to get up for work the next day!

Like equality, freedom has a number of definitions. It is another contested concept which is sometimes easier to use than to define precisely. One of the most important distinctions is that between 'freedom to' and 'freedom from'. Margaret Atwood writes in her novel, *The Handmaid's Tale*: 'There is more than one kind of freedom, said Aunt Lydia. Freedom to and freedom from. In the days of anarchy, it was freedom to. Now you are being given freedom from. Don't underrate it' (Atwood, 1985, p.34).

In Margaret Atwood's dystopian vision of the future women are given *freedom from* their own sexuality – to a degree at least, in as much as sexual relations are strongly regulated. On the other hand, they are given the *freedom to* walk down the street without fear of being sexually assaulted. This distinction between 'freedom to' and 'freedom from' is often understood through the terms 'positive freedom' and 'negative freedom', first used by the philosopher, Isaiah Berlin, in his famous essay 'Two concepts of liberty', and discussed in Vivienne Brown's chapter in this volume as well as in Chapter 5. In Berlin's view negative freedom is concerned with the extent to which a person is able to act without obstruction. This implies only obstructions which are the result of deliberate acts by states or by other human beings. What this means is that 'mere incapacity to attain a goal is not lack of political freedom' (Berlin, 1997, p.393; first published 1958).

However, it would seem to many that the fact that I have the freedom to buy a mansion in as much as nobody prevents me from doing so, is not the same as being able to buy a mansion. To be formally free and yet still constrained by social circumstances is what social justice is mainly concerned with. For example, women are formally equal, and yet statistics tell us that they are still paid, on average, less than men for doing the same type of work. Men and women are formally equal in the workplace, that is they have the same rights and protections, yet many more women than men are sexually harassed.

The idea of liberty is often contrasted with equality. This argument is often presented as a conflict; we must choose one or the other, or at the very least we must choose to prioritize one rather than the other. However, as Steven Lukes (1991) has argued, this is to set up a false tension. The arguments used to support this notion of an irreconcilable conflict are usually based on a misunderstanding of the values of liberty and equality. Libertarians tend to

conceive of liberty in such a way that it is by definition irreconcilable with
equality. For example, they suggest that any move toward greater equality
must result in less freedom; they conceptualize equality rather narrowly as
'equality of outcome' (i.e. 'to each the same amount'). They then move from
this to an argument that equality means 'fair shares for all'. This being the
case, somebody must decide what are fair shares and this means that we must
cede some of our liberty to the person, or committee, or state making the
decision about what is fair. Hence, equality must mean a reduction in our
liberty. But, as Lukes points out, few people argue for either equality of
outcome as it is described by libertarians or for fair shares for all as decided
by some central committee. Joel Feinberg (1980) makes the point that, in any
case, the distinction between 'freedom from' and 'freedom to' is probably a
false dichotomy too, in as much as the two are logically connected. People, in
general, do want the freedom to acquire material well-being, but at the same
time they want freedom from excessive interference with their liberty. People
also want a measure of equality, not equality of outcome perhaps, but
equality of opportunity, equality of rights, and equality of respect.

SUMMARY

- Liberty and equality are often seen to be in conflict.
- Negative freedom is defined as 'freedom from' whilst positive
  freedom is 'freedom to'.
- Lukes argues that the idea that liberty and equality are in conflict is
  based on a false dichotomy, derived from false premises.

6   A PLURALIST ACCOUNT OF EQUALITY

As we have seen, equality can mean different things. Amartya Sen (1992) says that one of the most important questions facing egalitarians is 'equality of what?' Sen's argument is that all theories of social justice imply equality of some sort, at some level. For egalitarians the type of equality concerned is usually spelled out very clearly. For Rawls, for example, it is concerned with equal liberty, for others it might be about equality of treatment and resources, or equality of income. Even those opposed to certain forms of equality call on the principle in some way. Nozick, for example, 'does demand equality of libertarian rights – no one has any more right to liberty than anyone else' (Sen, 1992, p.13). Just as Nozick argues that egalitarian writers are forced to concede pluralism, so Sen argues that libertarians are forced to concede the moral power of equality.

This is not just a theoretical issue. Indeed, equality – particularly equality of opportunity – is high on the policy agenda. Many equal opportunities policies are based on the 'politics of difference'. They 'seek to transform organizations and create a culture of diversity in which people of a much broader range of characteristics and backgrounds may contribute and flourish' (Rees, 1998, p.27). In other words, the power of equality has by no means diminished in the public eye, and that is a problem for anti-egalitarians. It is also a problem for egalitarians in as much as the failure to take account of different forms of equality can be confusing for practitioners and the failure to deliver what people expect from equality policies can lead to disillusionment and even outright hostility (Jewson and Mason, 1986).

This plurality or multiplicity of ways of thinking about equality (and of being equal) goes to the heart of the work of a third major contemporary theorist of justice, Michael Walzer, whose *Spheres of Justice* (1983) attempts a pluralist defence of equality. What this means is that there is no one single unitary way of devising justice, that justice requires a plurality of different principles operating in different spheres according to different rules. This is a clear attempt to reconcile equality with difference.

For Walzer, there is no point in pursuing simple equality ('to each the same amount'). This might be appropriate for some goods, but different goods require different principles, such as merit, effort, or need. For Walzer, complex societies, such as our contemporary ones, have different criteria for distributing different goods. He considers a wide variety of examples of 'goods' that societies distribute to members, including membership, welfare, 'money and commodities', office, hard work (by which he means physically hard work), free time, education, 'kinship and love', divine grace, recognition and political power. In Walzer's view, such goods constitute 'spheres', and justice is different in one sphere to the next. The criterion for the distribution of health care, for example, will not be the same as for the distribution of divine grace or political power. The criteria for distributing goods come from the meanings of those goods shared by the members of that society. If, for example, access to health care is widely understood in a society as properly distributed according to need (as opposed, say, to status), then need ought to be the criterion for distributing that good. This is a challenge to Rawls's view of the primary good, for, as Walzer argues, the same good might have different meanings at different times. 'A single necessary good, and one that is always necessary – food, for example – carries different meanings in different places. Bread is the staff of life, the body of Christ, the symbol of the Sabbath, the means of hospitality, and so on' (Walzer, 1983, p.8). As Walzer notes, the same good can have different meanings, and which meaning is dominant depends on the cultural setting. A good in this view might be primary in one sphere at one time or another, but not in another. All goods must, therefore, be seen through the prism of the community of which they form a part. Sometimes this approach is called 'communitarian' for this sort of reason, as opposed to the 'liberal' view of Rawls and the 'libertarian' view of Nozick, for example.

In this way, Walzer argues for a pluralistic account of justice, defined by what he calls '*complex equality*'. Put simply, complex equality argues that 'no citizen's standing in one sphere or with regard to one social good can be undercut by his standing in some other sphere, with regard to some other good' (Walzer, 1983, p.19). For example, just because someone is doing well in the sphere of money or commodities, or in terms of their professional status, it does not mean that they should have superior access to health care or education or social services. *Within* any one sphere, there may be inequality. That, in Walzer's view, is not necessarily unjust. Injustice kicks in when there is 'boundary-crossing' from one sphere to another or others. The important thing, from Walzer's perspective, is that inequalities should be confined within their sphere and should not distort the distributions within other spheres, which are achieved according to different distributive criteria. Let us say, for example, that in the political sphere office is distributed according to votes cast. All citizens have one vote and nobody's vote counts for more than any one else's vote. Votes cannot be bought and sold. Now, once the votes have been cast and counted, one citizen will emerge as the winner and thus the equal distribution of votes will create an unequal outcome. Not everybody can be an MP, not everybody wants to be. Walzer's point is that this inequality should not spill over into other spheres, so that being successful in the political sphere should not, for example, give unequal access to health care or education. The distribution of health care should still be on the basis of need, the distribution of examination grades on the basis of desert.

Liberals and others have been critical of Walzer's arguments. Some suggest that he uses standards of social justice that are too close to actual practices in societies – they lack a 'critical distance' from everyday political and economic life, and end up by endorsing what happens to be done anyway. Other critics suggest that Walzer's theory of justice is 'relativist': it does not provide us with a way of saying what justice really is, separate from particular places and cultures. Walzer might reply that there is no single or superior point of view from which we can see what justice is, separate from our everyday existences. According to his argument, we *create* our standards and theories of justice, we do not *discover* something finished and pristine that was already there.

SUMMARY

- Sen argues that all theories of justice have to answer the question 'equality of what?'
- Walzer's account of social justice aims to be both pluralistic and egalitarian.
- Complex equality recognizes that different goods have different meanings according to their cultural usage.

7 CONCLUSION: DIFFERENT BUT EQUAL?

It is undoubtedly the case that what Walzer designates 'simple equality' – straightforward, blanket levelling of goods and opportunities – does not seem to take account of our basic intuitions about the value of equality. If everybody is to have equal shares of everything then where is the place for our differences to emerge? What is the point in putting in effort if that effort is not going to be rewarded? Why should our unique talents not be recognized? Any scheme of social justice must take account of these questions. Nevertheless, we might want to argue for simple or strong equality in some spheres of our lives, for example with regard to our political and social rights. Perhaps this is one reason why the distinction between 'equality' and 'difference' is not always as helpful as it might first appear. The question is not so much whether we are different or equal, but how, given our differences, can we (and should) be equal? In terms of having the same rights, perhaps? Or similar levels of wealth or income? Or in a more pluralistic and complex set of domains, as Walzer might have it?

As Iris Young (1990) points out, we are accustomed to thinking about differences between social groups more than those between individuals. Social justice is primarily concerned with distribution, but there is no reason why it should not embrace the feminist slogan 'the personal is political' and deal with a range of other cultural issues as well. Indeed, if the primary cause of injustice is relations between persons, it might well be that an emphasis on distribution could produce formal equality but leave in place substantial social inequality, for example with respect to the social status and opportunities afforded to women in society, unfair discrimination against people who are members of minority ethnic or religious groups, or against disabled people or some minority sexual groups (see **Squires, 2005,** and **Watson, 2005,** for useful discussions of these issues). In this sense, difference is often about social and cultural differences and identities (sexual, religious, ethnic, and so on), as well as differences in material means.

The search for social justice is not a search for something that is there, already made, awaiting discovery. It is something that we make *by* searching for it. New critics introduce new ways for us to search; for example, feminist theorists in recent decades showed how social justice should not be built on arguments that assumed 'individuals' in an undifferentiated way, when the traditional liberal individual is in fact built around a traditional male model. There is no evidence that women are any less talented or less prone to putting in effort, and yet across many societies and social classes women's lives are constructed in ways which direct them first and foremost toward a caring role, whilst men are given far more opportunities to develop their interests.

The theorists discussed in this chapter have offered influential and much-debated ideas, some of which have influenced policy makers in both the UK and the USA. According to Rawls, we should all share a vision of justice which balances liberty, equality and different outcomes. Nozick, on the other hand, regards our differences as so fundamental that we cannot hope to create a society that would suit everybody. Moreover, from his point of view, strong versions of equality rely on constant obstruction of our rights to liberty by a heavy-handed, interfering state. For Walzer, the 'difference' lies in different goods forming different spheres with different distributive criteria.

'Social justice' remains a living political idea with strong appeal. The role of political theory is to push forward the debate and to bring these ideas to life, by lending them a precision they may well lack in popular discourse.

REFERENCES

Atwood, M. (1985) *The Handmaid's Tale*, London, Jonathan Cape.

Berlin, I. (1997; first published 1958) 'Two concepts of liberty' in Goodin, R.E. and Pettit, P. (eds) *Contemporary Political Philosophy. An Anthology*, Oxford, Blackwell.

Doyal, L. and Gough, I. (1991) *A Theory of Human Need*, Basingstoke, Macmillan.

Dworkin, R. (1977) *Taking Rights Seriously*, London, Duckworth.

Edwards, J. (1995) *When Race Counts. The Morality of Racial Preference in Britain and America*, London, Routledge.

Feinberg, J. (1980) *Rights, Justice and the Bounds of Liberty*, Princeton, NJ, Princeton University Press.

Freeden, M. (2003) *Ideology: a Very Short Introduction*, Oxford, Oxford University Press.

Hayek, F.A. (1976; first published 1944) *The Road to Serfdom*, Chicago, University of Chicago Press.

Heller, A. (1987) *Beyond Justice*, Cambridge, Basil Blackwell.

Jewson, N. and Mason, D. (1986) 'The theory and practice of equal opportunities policies: liberal and radical perspectives', *Sociological Review*, vol.34, no.2, pp.307–33.

Joseph, K. and Sumption, J. (1979) *Equality*, London, John Murray.

Lukes, S. (1991) 'Equality and liberty' in Held, D. (ed.) *Political Theory Today*, Cambridge, Polity Press.

Miller, D. (1976) *Social Justice*, Oxford, Oxford University Press.

Mitchell, J. (2005) 'Analysing politics: constitutional reform' in Heffernan, R. and Thompson, G. (eds) *Politics and Power in the UK*, Edinburgh, Edinburgh University Press/The Open University.

Nozick, R. (1974) *Anarchy, State and Utopia*, Oxford, Blackwell.

Nussbaum, M. (2001) 'The enduring significance of John Rawls' in *The Chronicle of Higher Education*, 20 July.

Perelman, C. (1963) *The Idea of Justice and the Problem of Argument*, London, Routledge and Kegan Paul.

Rawls, J. (1971) *A Theory of Justice*, Oxford, Oxford University Press.

Rawls, J. (2001) *Justice as Fairness*, Cambridge, Mass., Harvard University Press.

Rees, T. (1998) *Mainstreaming Equality in the European Union*, London, Routledge.

Sen, A. (1992) *Inequality Re-examined*, Oxford, Oxford University Press.

Squires, J. (2005) 'Common citizenship and plural identities: the politics of social difference' in Lewis, P. (ed.) *Exploring Political Worlds*, Edinburgh, Edinburgh University Press/The Open University.

Walzer, M. (1983) *Spheres of Justice. A Defence of Pluralism and Equality*, Oxford, Blackwell.

Watson, N. (2005) 'Fair policy or special treatment?: disability politics' in Prokhovnik, R. (ed.) *Making Policy, Shaping Lives*, Edinburgh, Edinburgh University Press/The Open University.

Young, I.M. (1990) *Justice and the Politics of Difference*, Princeton, NJ, Princeton University Press.

FURTHER READING

Kymlicka, W. (1990) *Contemporary Political Philosophy*, Oxford, Clarendon Press.

Mulhall, S. and Swift, A. (1996) *Liberals and Communitarians* (2nd edn), Oxford, Blackwell.

Wolff, J. (1996) *An Introduction to Political Philosophy*, Oxford, Oxford University Press.

Using theory

Mark J. Smith

Contents

Evidence & argument

1   INTRODUCTION

We have come a long way in a short time in this book's journey through selected living political ideas. Recall where we started: with the overarching category of the living political idea itself. Ideas live: they change and adapt, fade and revive, attract and repel. We have found this to be true of different sorts of political ideas. Political theories, such as the theories of state legitimacy, are all about contestation and adaptation. Notice how, for example, the social contract theory approach from the classics of Hobbes, Locke and Rousseau was revived and transformed two or three hundred years later by John Rawls. Ideologies, too, change and adapt. And political concepts are used and disputed in different ways in different eras. Struggles over the meanings of concepts are a core part of raw power politics too. This is another sense in which political ideas 'live' – people live or suffer the consequences of ideas being put into practice in the design of institutions and the making of policy.

In this chapter we will draw some threads together in the discussion of ideas, theory and ideology. I start with the differences between explanatory and normative political theory and their relationship to the much broader category of political science. Various issues about facts and values in the study of political theory will arise. I will also cover the contested character of concepts, before moving on to consider the character of political ideology as it has emerged in other chapters. Finally, I will look at the links *between* political theory (especially normative political theory) and political ideology, asking just how different they are, and how they may overlap and relate to each other. The theme of evidence and argument is woven through all of these topics. Ideas, theories and ideologies are all about constructing effective arguments, and assessing what counts as a good argument, among students of politics, and politicians and activists. Arguments about, for example, political legitimacy, nationalism, social justice and so on, grew out of different theories, frameworks and approaches. At one level, the study of ideas *is* the study of such arguments, and the forms of evidence they evoke. Among other examples, in this chapter I shall return to the different views of freedom which have been mentioned in both Chapters 1 and 4 to illustrate some of these competing perspectives further.

Just as theories and ideologies represent different sorts of arguments, calling on different sorts of evidence and frameworks, so concepts are essentially contested. As such they are better understood by focusing on their relations with other concepts – for example, social contract theorists, as we saw in Chapter 1, linked the concept of 'political legitimacy' with that of 'obligation' to obey the state. In this way, political legitimacy gained the meaning the social contract theorists wanted it to have, precisely by being linked with obligation and other related concepts. When looked at this way, we can say that one task of political theory is to provide a *toolbox* for clarifying the meaning of concepts and how they are constructed. I will pursue this analogy further later in the chapter.

Political theory, which sometimes presents itself as above politics or politically neutral, cannot be divorced from the cut and thrust of political life and political argument. It is here, perhaps, that we can say that political ideologies, too, put concepts together in certain ways to a certain effect. If political theory provides a *toolbox*, ideologies often provide the *workbench* and a degree of urgency to get on with the job (because there is a world to be changed). Sometimes ideologies might even be seen as theories that are adapted to day-to-day political argument (though this applies less to the distinctive Marxist view of 'ideology' discussed in the Introduction and elsewhere). To study the uses of ideas in concrete political practices (as *living* political ideas) we are forced to conclude that the meaning of concepts is often produced by use rather than following the systematic prescriptions of well-known political theorists, such as Hobbes, Locke and Rawls. In this chapter I will look at selected ideologies and processes of ideological change to illustrate this point, and to explore the expansion and contraction of ideological debate, and the fast-changing and sometimes hybrid character of many ideologies. So, in addition to the toolbox provided by political theories, to understand how concepts and ideas are used we also need the workbench provided by the study of political ideologies.

SUMMARY

This chapter will:

- draw together some threads of discussions of ideas, theory, ideology and concepts found in previous chapters

- discuss the relationships of explanation and recommendation in political theory

- illustrate how concepts such as liberty get defined and incorporated into political ideologies

- explore the relationships, including continuities, between theory and ideology.

2 POLITICAL SCIENCE AND POLITICAL THEORY

Political science has often focused on attempts to describe how the political system actually operates, who makes the decisions, and how they justify these decisions in debates and public statements. What we might call 'close description' is a common form of writing in political science. The focus is on the observable politics of national assemblies, party debate, media campaigns and so on. Sometimes political scientists go further, not only concerned with good descriptions but seeking also to *explain* political events and phenomena. To do this, they need a theory of why things happen, what causes change. Perhaps the three most common explanatory theories used by political scientists are: (a) the rational choice model, (b) the functional model and (c) the interpretative model.

Rational choice theorists explain political events by starting with an assumption that all people are out to maximize their utility. This means that they are self-interested, and will choose the most effective path to whatever goals they happen to have. Thus, for example, rational choice approaches suggest hypotheses such as that voters vote for the party that will benefit them most personally, and that politicians advocate those policies that are most likely to get them into office (rather than the ones they think are good or right otherwise). Functional explanations, on the other hand, offer hypotheses which suggest that events occur because there is a need for them in the larger system of which they are a part. For example, Marxism is sometimes viewed as a functional approach, suggesting that proletarian revolution necessarily develops in capitalist societies to transform the great pressures that the contradictions of capitalism provoke. Interpretivist explanations seek to explain events by getting inside the heads of participants, seeing how they produce meanings in specific contexts, seeing events from their perspective and in the light of their values and beliefs. Foucauldian approaches to explanation might broadly be seen as of this type, though they view meanings as regulated by discourses rather than the product of 'knowing' individuals.

I will not pursue further these modes of explanation in this chapter. The most common approaches to political theory we have encountered in this book are not meant primarily to *explain*. Rather, they are *normative* theories, in the sense that they *recommend* or *prescribe* courses of action. They are about the *ought*, rather than the *is*. Normative political theorists are preoccupied with *what ought to be*. They construct arguments about such issues as the proper role and size of the state, the nature of democracy and justice, individual responsibilities of citizens, and so on.

Explanatory approaches in political science and normative political theory do not occupy different universes, though. There is nothing about normative political theory which means that it is 'too abstract' or divorced from the real world of politics, accusations that are sometimes levelled at it. Consider this exchange, very much of the real world of politics and a concrete political situation, during prime minister's questions (17 December 2003) in the UK House of Commons.

Mr Michael Howard (Folkestone and Hythe) (Con): Can the Prime Minister tell us how much the cost of running central Government has increased since 1997?

The Prime Minister: The percentage of administration costs in central Government is actually lower than it was in 1997.

Mr Howard: So the Prime Minister does not know how much it costs to run his Government. It is £20 billion. That is nearly £7 billion more than in 1997. I am surprised that he does not know because I gave him the figures five weeks ago. Can he tell us now how many more civil servants are employed by central Government compared with 1997?

The Prime Minister: There are fewer civil servants than there were, for example, 10 years ago, but it is correct that recently numbers have increased – in the Prison Service and to deal with pensions and immigration issues. But overall, as I said a moment ago, the actual percentage costs of administration are lower now than they were in 1997.

Mr Howard: The answer is that there are 47,000 more civil servants in central Government compared not with 10 years ago, but with 1997. It is as many people as HSBC employs in the whole of the United Kingdom. So the Prime Minister does not know how much his Government cost or how many people they employ. Could he now give us the figure in the pre-Budget report – perhaps the Chancellor will help him – for Government spending on inspectors, regulators, paymasters and policy makers?

The Prime Minister: First, I repeat that the cost of administration as a percentage of central Government spending has actually gone down, not up, under this Government. Secondly, perhaps the right hon. and learned Gentleman will tell us how many of the additional prison officers, for example, he would cut, given the need to increase prison numbers – remembering, of course, that when he was Home Secretary he cut the numbers of police officers on Britain's streets. With regard to the Gershon report, yes there is £9 billion for central Government, but that includes the primary care trusts, the Food Standards Agency, Ofsted and the Prison Service. If he disagrees with that, how many jobs in such bodies would he cut?

Mr Howard: Let me remind the Prime Minister that this is Prime Minister's questions. I will make the Prime Minister an offer. If he wants me to answer the questions, let him give me a slot every week for Leader of the Opposition's questions. I would be very pleased to do that. He can choose the day – any day of the week – and I will be very pleased to answer his questions. But, just for the moment, he is still Prime Minister: it is my job to ask him questions and it is his duty to answer them.

(Hansard, 2003)

FIGURE 5.1   Michael Howard, Leader of the Opposition, in the House of Commons, December 2003

On one level, the political scientist will be interested in the political knockabout of prime minister's questions, the rhetorical and tactical moves the players can make to try to get some advantage in the exchanges, and so on. The political 'roles' of prime minister and leader of the opposition, how these have evolved and how they are played out in day-to-day politics, are also of interest. This discussion focuses on the administrative cost of the civil service to the taxpayer, with Michael Howard comparing the inefficiency of the state with the value for money that can be achieved in the private sector. The prime minister, Tony Blair, replies by using an alternative measure of efficiency – the cost of administration as a percentage of government spending. From such extracts we can gain a better understanding of the conduct of political debate, the attempt to score points, make one's opponent uncomfortable and construct statements that can be used as sound-bites for news broadcasts.

Descriptive or explanatory political science is very good at providing us with explanations of the institutional context of this debate: parliament, the party system, the presence of the prime minister (representing the executive) in the legislature, and the conventions that underpin the UK constitution. Political scientists in this respect focus on concrete decisions by observable political actors in definite institutional locations such as government, national assemblies or local political bodies. There is more going on in this extract from prime minister's questions, though. The exchange between Blair and Howard is also an exchange or contest about values, and indeed a contest over living political ideas.

Students of political ideology would be interested in what this exchange says about the ideologies of the leaders and their parties. Clearly, the role of government, and the legitimate size of the state, appear to be points of ideological dispute. I say this because an ideological dispute is more than a dispute about facts; it is about worldviews or outlooks, the kinds of framework or lens that we use when we try to interpret and make sense of the world, as well as form our opinions on how it might be made better. But political ideas are here in another form as well. Normative political theorists might look at the ways in which normative concepts are used, and to assess whether they are used by politicians. For example, a key concept here is 'efficiency' and theorists can clarify what this means. Concepts are singular, but conceptions can be plural.

Howard is articulating a conception of efficiency that stresses value for money (the delivery on objectives at the minimum cost), whereas Blair is concerned with the efficient delivery of public services at the point of use (to fulfil social objectives). Theorists can also highlight how these contested uses of the concept of 'efficiency' are based on a broader set of beliefs about how the political system, and how the country, should be run. Howard thinks that an efficient state is a minimal state that does not interfere more than is necessary in the private lives of citizens. In this sense, his views could be said to chime with the larger theory of social justice set out by Robert Nozick (see Chapter 4). However, Blair advocates a more interventionist state in order to deliver certain social goals in health and education; what he is arguing might well fit into a more social democratic notion of social justice as expounded by John Rawls, for example. The relationships between political debates and well-known normative political theories are not so straightforward, of course; I am offering illustrations here rather than a full-blown argument. The point is that political theory is concerned with exploring the normative questions raised by power, liberty, justice and the relationship between rights and obligations in contemporary political communities. Simply because normative political theorists try to take a step back from day-to-day politics to look at the structure of arguments themselves, does not mean those arguments and theories are not very much *political*. In addition, many political theorists have been willing to advocate their perspectives beyond academic institutions in the political debates that raged around them.

SUMMARY

- Political theory can be explanatory or normative.
- Normative political theory is concerned with how the state should be organized rather than with describing or explaining events.
- Normative political theory is not divorced from everyday politics, but rather can be used to help to make sense of *ought* arguments that are part of such politics.

3 NORMATIVE THEORIES, CONCEPTS AND POLITICS

Normative political theories are *prescriptive*; they suggest that there are problems in the way we organize ourselves and often put forward ways of constructing a better world. They attempt to clarify the criteria by which we judge whether a particular decision or policy is the right course of action. Utilitarians, for example, are concerned with calculating the consequences of political actions in their search to see the greatest happiness of the greatest number, or in more contemporary language, to maximize individual utility. Social contract theorists, on the other hand, and especially John Rawls, are more concerned with developing rules that all rational people could agree to, and which can apply to all. To offer one more example, communitarians, such as Michael Walzer (see Chapter 4), look to specific countries or communities and to the shared understandings about right and justice and so on which can be found there. Communitarians value principles and practices *because* they are the principles and practices of *these* people in *this* place.

These theories clash in their basic character, assumptions and prescriptions. Take the examples of utilitarianism and social contract approaches. Even though they are both liberal theories (as opposed to Marxist or absolutist, for example), at the most basic levels there are disagreements. According to utilitarians, one should calculate the pain and pleasure (in today's terminology, the costs and benefits) of a decision or policy. In this calculus, when pleasure is in excess of pain then a *prudent* decision would be to implement the proposal in order to maximize utility, that is satisfaction. Some members of the political community may indeed suffer from a decision but their loss can be seen as outweighed by the benefits for the many. Contractarian critics claim that utilitarianism treats individuals as a means rather than an end, and that this undervalues human beings. Such critics propose an alternative normative stance where individuals are ends in themselves and should be respected as such; that the right course of action will apply to everyone in the same way and that some members of the society in question should not suffer for the sake of the greatest good for the greatest number.

Normative political theory has thus produced intense discussions on, for example, whether political decisions should focus on the consequences that follow from our actions, or direct their attention to setting up a fair system of rules instead. The political setting of ends and decisions on the means to realize these ends is a process which often involves drawing on assumptions from competing political theories and using them to justify the actions involved.

Such contests can be seen as having a bearing on specific policy debates. Consider one here. Many cities and some countries are considering a ban on smoking in public spaces such as bars, restaurants and shops. To some extent this has been implemented in many workplaces and on public transport, and in the creation of no-smoking zones. There is considerable evidence of a decline in smoking, from it being the recreational habit of the majority to being a minority pastime (though some social groups have a higher proportion of regular smokers). The argument in favour of the ban is based on the scientific case that many non-smokers are at risk from illnesses caused by passive smoking. It is constructed on utilitarian grounds, taking into account the costs and benefits of smoker and non-smoker citizens as well as the collective benefits that can result from the consequences of an expected decline in smoking-related illnesses (for example, fewer patients with lung cancer and/or heart disease as well as a decline in absences from work as a result of chest complaints).

FIGURE 5.2 Smoking bans: putting theory into practice?

Some US cities, such as New York, have banned smoking in public places but have allowed for the continuation of a small number of cigar bars; these are strictly regulated, especially in relation to the risks for employees. Smoking-rights advocates believe that there is a variety of recreational drugs that have the potential for harm (to oneself and others) for which a ban is not anticipated (such as alcohol) and that, as a group, they have already been unfairly singled out through the imposition of high taxes on cigarettes. For them, individuals have rights, including rights over what they do with their own bodies. The very nature of a 'right' is that it is not to be overridden. What is right or fair for the anti-smoking lobby is perceived as wrong or unfair by defenders of smokers. It is always difficult to reconcile the principle of fairness with ensuring the greatest good for the greatest number, so policies involve a delicate balancing act between them.

Although the advocates of specific political theories will argue that their approach is the better way, to understand questions of justice it is always best to entertain a healthy sense of doubt. In practice, the application of political ideas can be a partial and complex business. In many ways, as suggested above, normative political theory is best treated as a *toolbox* for understanding actual political processes and relationships, as well as for getting to grips with the vocabularies used in political institutions. As Charles Lemert argues, we should not regard 'theory' as the preserve of 'experts'!

> Theory is a basic survival skill. This may surprise those who believe it to be a special activity of experts of a certain kind. True, there are professional theorists, usually academics. But this fact does not exclude my belief that ... theory is something done necessarily and often well by people with no professional credentials. When it is done well, by whomever, it can be a source of uncommon pleasure.
>
> (Lemert, 1993, p.1)

In short, we can treat theory as a kind of Swiss army knife, serving to uncork, chop into pieces, cut through and prise out what political agents really mean when they use concepts such as rights, obligations, freedom and so on. Are such concepts used consistently by the speaker or writer? Does the underlying argument make sense, not just as a piece of surface rhetoric? Core political concepts such as equality, obligation, freedom, social justice, democracy and so on, can indeed be treated and used differently by different politicians and observers. I turn to an example of this in the following section.

SUMMARY

- Debates in normative political theory focus on what is good and right.

- Normative political theory presents us with a lens for looking through issues where individual freedom and the greater good may clash, e.g. smoking.

4   MAKING SENSE OF CONCEPTS: THE EXAMPLE OF 'FREEDOM'

To make sense of the use of a concept such as freedom, we need to look carefully at how it is *defined* and how it is *combined* with other concepts. Let's look at two commonplace and conflicting uses of the concept of freedom as an example. First, positive liberty, freedom as the capacity to pursue one's own goals. This is sometimes expressed as 'freedom to'. Many argue that accepting the importance of positive liberty means accepting that the role of the state is to foster the conditions in which all individuals can use their capacities to pursue their own interests.

The aim is to achieve social objectives, with the investment in human capital designed to enhance the productivity of a population. Not only do individuals benefit from this investment, the whole society reaps the dividends. In short, the degree of freedom we enjoy depends on our social and economic resources.

The second use is negative liberty, freedom as the absence of restrictions on one's behaviour. This is sometimes expressed as 'freedom from', for example, the freedom from external constraint. The idea here is that you are free unless someone is actively preventing you from doing something. Often, accepting negative freedom is taken to mean accepting that the state's role is not to provide people with resources or foster their developing capacities, but rather just to leave them alone.

Negative liberty does place limits on the freedom to act; individuals are free to act so long as they do not infringe the liberties of others. This definition of freedom has been articulated with free market views of the economy and notions of personal responsibility. You have seen these assumptions in Brown's outline of Locke's constitutionalism and Middleton's discussion of Nozick's theory of justice (Chapters 1 and 4). The notion of positive freedom, on the other hand, is resonant of, for example, Rawls's difference principle, discussed by Middleton in Chapter 4.

Brown and Middleton both highlight the standpoint of Isaiah Berlin, a political theorist and historian of ideas, who famously set up the contrast between negative and positive freedom (though he sometimes used the word liberty). His aim is not to endorse one and reject the other but to point to the dangers of both (Berlin, 1969).

FIGURE 5.3   Isaiah Berlin

Berlin is most concerned with how positive freedom can become a cloak for repression. The difficulties start when we look at how 'being one's own master' has been understood. You will remember Brown's outline of Rousseau (Chapter 1, Section 2.3). If we imagine that humans enjoy natural freedom in the state of nature (Rousseau's *noble savage*), then the answer is to construct a political system in which all are governed by the general will which encompasses everyone's basic and common interests. All are assumed to have the same core needs and desires. Berlin questions this assumption, suggesting that the competing and diverse values and virtues that face individuals have been ignored in such accounts. When this happens, where *individual self-determination has been replaced by collective self-rule*, then from the Jacobins through to communism, authoritarianism inevitably follows.

Similar dilemmas are explored by Saward in Chapter 2 when considering the self-determination of people and the idea of a nation as a kind of 'self' determining its own existence and future. Nationalist projects draw on analogies and metaphors that attempt to invoke a *common* past and future, assuming that the 'nation' has self-awareness, territoriality, history and culture, language and religion. Nationalist movements often neglect the possibility that many groups, such as minorities (the Quebecois in Canada) and indigenous people (the Inuit in Canada) may have different ideas about collective identity. One should also remember Saward's point that the collective self-determination of the Quebecois will also create new minorities that do not share the values and assumptions of Quebec nationalists. This reinforces Berlin's point, that social orders are composed of competing and possible irreconcilable values and assumptions. In short, we should be sceptical of the benefits of collective self-rule for this often means individual rights may be violated. Positive freedom might go too far as a political programme; it may encourage political figures to try to iron out too much pluralism and difference, something that Berlin constantly emphasized.

So far we have concentrated on Berlin's worries about positive freedom. Negative freedom also has its problems, for it runs the risk of failing to protect the vulnerable. Even when there is an absence of constraints, people may be unaware of their options, or not have access to resources to enable them to act on their choices.

Rather than seeing these concepts of freedom as fundamentally distinct, Berlin concludes that both positive and negative freedom are necessary for a decent existence and both are undermined if our capacity to make choices is impaired. Moreover, he suggests that there is a tendency to construct a perfectly rational actor as the basis of political theories when, in fact, we need to think in terms of individuals trying to muddle through with inconsistent and conflicting values where the options are not always clear. Why should we assume that individuals would want to live a good and virtuous life as someone else would define it? He advocated, in other words, moral pluralism, and aspects of both negative and positive freedom could be friend and foe to an open and pluralist society (Berlin, 1969; Gray, 1995).

So we have seen that important concepts can be understood in quite distinct ways; and that those ways have consequences when understood in terms of the roles of states. We have also seen that sometimes these distinctions do not seem so clear cut. This, too, is part of what it means to explore living political ideas.

Note that a specific way of defining one concept can be associated with specific ways of defining *other* concepts. And, in turn, a set of concepts given a particular, consistent 'spin' could make up a theory. Consider how another core political concept, equality, can be understood in different ways in relation to the two major characterizations of freedom that we have just introduced.

- *Equality of opportunity*, where it is equal chances or starting points that count. Here, the argument involves the state providing additional support for the underprivileged so that they might compete on equal terms with others; equality of opportunity may be compatible with inequality of outcome or rewards.

- *Equality of outcome*, where all get the same material rewards at the end of the day.

- *Formal equality before the law*, where the state has no specific role in supporting people or providing resources, but rather its role is to protect individual rights (including Lockean-style rights to property, for example).

Advocates of negative freedom suggest that equality of opportunity and/or outcome undermines the system of rewards that are necessary to motivate individuals to succeed; that individuals will not defer gratification and work hard for their goals if the rewards are non-existent or marginal later on. Instead, they argue, we should harness such effort by leaving people to follow their own interests, and as a result the society as a whole benefits. In this sense, they would favour a more narrow, formal conception of equality before the law. Advocates of positive freedom are more likely to support more substantial and interventionist notions of equality, such as strong versions of equality of opportunity and even equality of outcome.

We should not assume that the definitions of equality are mutually exclusive. Conservatives often claim that status differences based on *rank* and *merit* are compatible; that inequalities based on ascribed status such as inherited wealth do not lead to an ossified social order because the elite are refreshed by the upwardly mobile intelligent few that achieve their status through ability and effort (Bond and Saunders, 1999). Socialists have been known to combine recognition of *merit* with 'to each according to their *work*'. Equality and freedom are slippery concepts and we need to take care to think through how they are defined and how they are combined with other concepts to make political theories and political ideologies – themselves changeable, as are all living political ideas. We have seen ample evidence of this, not only in Berlin's work, but also that of classic theorists such as Locke and Rousseau and contemporaries such as Rawls and Nozick.

SUMMARY

● Political theories provide a toolbox for clarifying the meaning of concepts and for explaining and understanding political processes and relations.

● Careful analysis can reveal how the different uses of concepts cast light on the values and assumptions of political theorists themselves.

● Analysing the example of 'freedom' shows us how one concept can have a number of conceptions, and can be used in different theories.

5   IDEOLOGY AS A CONTESTED CONCEPT

Let us turn from this focus on normative political theory to political ideology. It is clear that the two have their similarities – for example, they both define and deploy concepts in distinctive ways. Ideologies, in the major contemporary sense of the term, are mainly intended to have a direct political effect – to change the world.

There is no one definitive statement on the meaning of ideology; its meaning depends very much on its use. We saw in the Introduction and in Chapters 1 and 2, for example, evidence of some of the different senses of ideology. At a very general level, ideologies are perspectives from which society can be viewed and politics can be conducted. Historically, it has had positive and negative connotations. The term *ideology* was originally devised in 1797 by Antoine Destutt de Tracy as a label for the 'science of ideas' – that if we can use rational thought to explain how society works then we can plan for a more orderly and peaceful existence; an answer to the problems created by the French Revolution. Within a short time Napoleon used it in a negative way to describe the 'scribbling ideologues' as unable to deal with practicalities of power politics.

These conflicting interpretations that have come to be associated with the word ideology go back much further and are briefly illustrated by two examples. Machiavelli (1469–1527) highlighted how force alone can be used successfully to control a population, the most important task of a ruler. In order to mobilize the friendship and goodwill of their subjects, princes needed to practice deceit and should be seen to be just even if they were not. Francis Bacon (1561–1626) warned against the dangers of trusting in idols that prevented objectivity. Bacon highlights four such idols: the tribe (the unquestioning belief in tradition and allowing one's passions to overcome reason), the cave (the limits of one's own partial experiences), the marketplace (the distortions of language and social discourse) and the theatre (dogmatic beliefs from the past). Of course, neither Machiavelli nor Bacon used the word ideology, but their respective accounts of the use of ideas to manipulate people and distort reality are present in many contemporary uses of the word.

Believers in a particular ideology tend to reserve such accusations of self-delusion and lack of objectivity for the holders of *other* ideologies. There is a degree of righteousness involved. Ideologies contain a belief about what the social and political order should be like, a belief that can sometimes be associated with a missionary zeal to convert new followers. Moreover, they are partial and partisan views about the organization of society. For those with strong commitment to a specific ideology, the values that underpin it may seem to be so self-evidently true they do not need much justification. Consider the two examples of political ideologies: conservatism and Marxism.

For those who identify strongly with *conservatism*, human nature is viewed pessimistically. In order to construct a stable and orderly society, individuals and groups need strict control (to avoid a 'war of all against all'). There is also a clear emphasis on tradition and the institutions that have emerged through trial and error. Tradition is seen as our ancestors voting in the present; refusing to submit to the 'arrogant oligarchy of those who merely happen to be walking about'. This is associated with myths of a tranquil past that has been shattered by shifting moral values and the behaviour of younger generations. One British conservative, Sir John Stokes, expressed this attitude by stating that 'the twentieth century has been a grotesque mistake'. Social change is viewed suspiciously and is often seen as unnecessary (or at least should be avoided until it is absolutely necessary) with gradual evolution grudgingly accepted.

Conservatism assumes that there is common commitment to certain cultural, specific core values of a particular society, embodied in phrases such as 'this is a free country' or 'equality under the law'. Conservatives place an emphasis on clearly defining statehood and ethnic or cultural identity, locating these in terms of a place with natural boundaries (see Chapter 2). For example, the philosopher Roger Scruton comments on how the physical landscape of the English countryside is a product of the historical compromises between different social groups. He draws attention to how public rights of way (evolving over centuries) are respected by the boundaries constructed to mark land ownership and building tenure. Even the construction of dry-stone walls around the patchwork quilt of fields facilitates organized fox hunting across private lands, a leisure activity that he argues symbolizes the development of social bonds of different social classes. For Scruton, the imaginary and symbolic aspects of cultural identity are represented through the literature, poetry, paintings and even the practices of voluntary associations (Scruton, 1984). As Saward suggests, the sense of belonging engendered by cultural or national identity is no less potent as a force for mobilizing consent. Scruton even goes so far as to suggest that the 'English' are most individualistic when they wear uniforms, whether these are the cricket team or a brass band, rugby club or church choir, as an emotional and sentimental expression of their common roots and cultural heritage.

The conservative position is often described as intuitive common sense rather than as ideology. Any abstract theory that does not draw on the lived experience of generations and seeks to wipe the slate clean and start again with the social order is 'ideological' and dangerous, from a conservative point of view. One interesting complication is that, if ideas that originate in liberal or even socialist thinking come to be embedded in a particular society, then conservatives will normally defend those social arrangements (such as an attachment to welfare systems and industrial participation). They believe it is better to trust in a system that works (despite its shortcomings) than place one's faith in a system that has not been subject to the test of experience. Radical change is dangerous precisely because it may undo the complex moral fabric that binds a society together; a moral fabric that works most effectively when it has evolved over time.

The operation of what Marxists refer to with the word 'ideology' is dependent on the economic organization of society; that the control of the means of material production or *base* (factories) creates the conditions for control of the means of mental production or *superstructure* (ideas). Ideology is thus an instrument of class domination. Bear in mind that, for Marxists, society is constituted by social classes. Bourgeois ideology (the worldview of the dominant or ruling class in a capitalist society) is dominant when the active consent of the social classes (such as the proletariat and the peasantry) and other social categories (such as intellectuals and bureaucrats) has been secured. Marxists were consummate storytellers using a range of devices and analogies to make their narrative plausible. The base–superstructure metaphor has been described in various ways, including a sailing ship: with the economy as the hull, the political system as the masts and rigging (for steering the society on its journey), ideology as the wind in the sails and philosophers in the crow's nest pointing in various directions. All these stories demonstrate how the organization of production is exploitative and at the same time ideologically camouflaged as a fair exchange in the marketplace conducted between free agents (see Figure 5.4).

Since a ruling class is not going to sacrifice its interests willingly, the generation of consent is reinforced by the use of force; consent and coercion work hand in hand. Karl Marx and Friedrich Engels believed that their analysis would lay bare the inner workings of the social and political order with the precision of a natural science, revealing the exploitative and oppressive system for what it was. This treatment of ideology established a series of moves to contrast science (in this case, scientific socialism) with ideology. A significant contributor, Antonio Gramsci, described ideology as a terrain where social forces engage and struggle for control (using the analogy of trench warfare). Rather than seeing consciousness as true or false, the members of a social order acquire consciousness of their position through economic, political and ideological struggle.

FIGURE 5.4

Let's put forward a definition of ideology in the light of the above discussion. An ideology is a set of ideas, concepts and norms which provides people with a way to understand the world and a guide to political action. Often, the term carries a negative connotation. We saw, for example, how both conservatives and Marxists described the worldviews of everyone else except themselves as ideological.

Often, ideologies such as conservatism, socialism and Marxism are contrasted to the dominant ideology of our time, liberalism. It is worth pausing to consider some key characteristics of liberalism, an ideology that permeates the institutional frameworks of all Western democratic societies, acting as the conceptual furniture of Western societies. It is primarily concerned with the means through which we achieve objectives without specifying what those ends should be. Even the utilitarian goal of maximizing happiness or utility (utilitarians and contract theorists are united in the sense that they are liberals) discussed above is a mechanism for calculating the respective goals that different people happen to have; it does not offer a vision of the good society beyond those varied, individual goals. In particular, liberalism asserts the importance of the freedom of individuals to construct their own lives in a context of legitimate but limited political authority.

For liberals, conflicts between individuals, groups, organizations and even states should be mediated by neutral institutions whose judgements apply to all ('rule by laws' is more just than 'rule by men'). Such rules should ensure that competing interests are reconciled or, that where grievances emerge, they can be reconciled via the impartial adjudication of the civil legal system. Societies need procedures and institutions through which competing interests and ideas are reconciled which are trusted by all the agents involved. It follows for many liberals that political decision making should follow from a free and fair debate between different viewpoints so that all sides feel adequately represented.

This is the basis for what Karl Popper described as the 'open society', where rules based on tolerance and open mindedness prevent intolerance and dogmatism. Popper's views on science and knowledge are closely linked to his ideas on the open society. In science (when constructing tests and using scientific laws), just as in everyday life, it is common to confirm what we already feel to be true and assume that things will always be the same. For Popper, progress was achieved by falsifying what we take for granted, forcing us to think harder rather than stagnate. In short, he argued that we need procedures for producing knowledge that maximize the potential for innovation but remains tolerant towards differences of opinion and belief. So, the truth should never be assumed and the best we can hope for is 'verisimilitude' (the best duplicate of the truth). We should always expect better versions to arise later. So too, in politics, it was the construction of institutions and rules that enabled all interested agents to engage in dialogue and have a say on decisions about society's objectives that created a free and democratic system. To behave intolerantly (in politics or knowledge) damages the process and undermines the open society (Popper, 1945).

So, unlike the conservative treatment of the *virus of ideology* (trust your instincts three times a day, if you think too hard or in abstract ways come back for a second appointment), liberals prescribe a full course of rational thinking with a supplement of scepticism (a healthy sense of doubt) to deal with any unwanted side-effects. Like conservatism, liberalism does not see itself as an ideology – a term that it associates with totalitarianism. We need to be cautious in using such labels. With the peculiar exception of Benito Mussolini, the label of 'totalitarian' is not one that has been endorsed by the advocates of specific political ideologies. It is a derogatory label for classifying political ideas which are viewed as contrary to liberal political ideas.

From a liberal point of view, deviation from liberal values leads towards authoritarian situations where the rights of individuals are sacrificed for some greater goal, such as military pushes for territorial expansion or the forced collectivization of production (as in Stalin's 'socialism in one country'). Totalitarianism is a liberal construct for classifying all political ideas that are fixated on the 'ends' and fail to construct the best 'means' through which individuals can realize their own ends.

So far we have seen that each ideology has a distinctive take on just who and what is ideological. Liberals, conservatives and Marxists have set up a contrast between their own core values and assumptions and those values and assumptions they regard as 'ideological': suspicious, distorting or downright dangerous.

SUMMARY

- Ideology has negative and positive connotations.
- Ideologies provide a belief system for political agents such as conservatives, liberals or Marxists that acts as a guide to action.
- All the ideologies covered in this section, in their different ways, see themselves as non-ideological, claiming they have an objective view of the social and political order.

6   GENDERED IDEOLOGIES

New ideologies tend to build on elements of existing ones even while they attempt to offer something new. Indeed, more generally we can say that ideologies are never totally coherent – in political practices we often mix up ideas, concepts and norms from different ideologies. The commitment of conservatives, liberals and many socialists to the idea of freedom reveals that constituent elements of ideologies are not mutually exclusive. The meaning of concepts such as equality, freedom, justice and so on depends on the framework of related concepts into which they are inserted.

In this section we will consider one more ideology that challenges 'ideology' – the feminist approach. We will also notice how feminism builds on elements of existing ideologies and overlaps in dynamic ways with them.

Feminism identifies a common feature in all the ideologies considered so far: androcentrism (male-centredness). Liberal values are grounded in a conception of rights and obligations of citizens endowed with rationality. But it arose in a cultural context in which it was believed that certain social groups did not possess the capacity for reason or lacked the virtues for civilized discourse: slaves and women. A tricky question arises. Does one challenge the argument that 'reason' is the entry ticket to these societies, or rather the assumption that these social groups do not possess it? Early feminist thinking took the latter route, asserting the capacity for reasoning that, according to Mary Wollstonecraft, had been fettered by the customary habits and duties assigned to her gender.

> I still insist that not only the virtue but the knowledge of the two sexes should be the same in nature, if not in degree, and that women, considered not only as moral but as rational creatures, ought to endeavour to acquire human virtues (or perfections) by the same means as men, instead of being educated like a fanciful kind of half being.
>
> (Wollstonecraft, 1975, p.125; first published 1792)

In addition, Wollstonecraft argued that the virtues and qualities ascribed to women in eighteenth-century Europe (such as modesty and chastity), as well as the virtues associated with masculinity, should all be seen as social virtues to which all individuals should aspire. Similarly, in the 1850s, for Harriet Taylor and John Stuart Mill, the exclusion of women from the public sphere (within which sovereign individuals enjoyed political, legal and economic rights) was contrary to the spirit of enlightenment reasoning and simply part of the dull weight of tradition. Moreover, Mill couched his arguments in utilitarian terms – that the emancipation of women would benefit the collective organization of society. This mix of arguments, based on utility and morals, was a feature of *first-wave* feminist interventions until the late twentieth century.

The suffrage movement, which aimed to win the right to vote for women, achieved its objectives, in part, because of its acceptance of the imperative of national efficiency alongside purity politics on issues such as health and prostitution (epitomized in the slogan 'votes for women, chastity for men'), but also for not challenging the distinction between the public and private spheres which has been a core part of liberalism. Simone de Beauvoir presented a similar ambivalent approach to the mind and body in *The Second Sex* (1972; first published 1949); that women's bodies made them amenable to being constructed as man's *Other* (sentenced to a life of passive embodiment weighed down by the peculiarities of the body for the uses of the male), inhibiting the attainment of a free and authentic self.

Feminist interventions from the 1960s challenged this fixation on the mind as liberation (based on the norms of a 'masculine subject') and the body as constraint for subscribing to male norms for defining freedom. Frustrated by the subsequent failures of formal legal reform (on divorce, equal pay, discrimination and so on) to generate actual equality, feminist approaches subjected the whole social order to a forensic examination. *Second-wave* feminism argued that the fundamental oppression was that based on patriarchy and one that permeated all institutions, whether in the public or private spheres (manifested in sexism and discrimination). For this account, unequal relations of power operated as much in the family, kinship networks, workplace and communities as it did in politics; a complex set of relations sustained through a 'patriarchal ideology' that systematically constrained women and distorted the personalities of both men and women (all individuals were victims of this exploitative and dehumanizing system). Like Marxism, feminism sought to draw on the standpoint of the oppressed group to construct an objective account of social organization (such as the technique of 'group consciousness-raising') and in identifying strategies for social and political transformation. This led to the conclusion that power operates in personal life in matters such as educational practices, domestic violence and sexual assault (that 'the personal is political'). In this analysis, patriarchal ideologies function to sustain gender inequality.

It is useful to draw some parallels between the transformational political ideas of Marxism and feminism. Both suggest the analysis of deeply embedded social and political structures to be oppressive and exploitative, rather than a natural part of the way things are done. This is combined with the belief that since human beings construct social structures, they can transform them through strategies for social change. Both approaches challenge the existing social and political system (they provide good examples of ideologies as vehicles for dissent, as discussed by Andrews in Chapter 3). Indeed, Marxist and feminist approaches were often combined, and in one version of this analysis (patriarchal capitalism) economic and gender inequalities are mutually reinforcing. Some of the most intense criticism arose from black feminism which accused white Western feminist strategies of being 'colour-blind' (Collins, 1990).

One of the difficulties with this approach was that feminists found considerable differences in experience, and that gender could not be considered in isolation from social class background, ethnic identity and matters of sexual preference. This raised questions about whether it was possible to identify underlying real interests with any degree of certainty and undermined the belief in a common source or universal existence of oppression. As a result, recent feminist studies have emphasized the need to focus on historically and culturally specific racisms, sexisms and heterosexisms (the precise form of gender oppression and combinations with other social antagonisms depending on the situation in question).

SUMMARY

- New ideologies tend to build partly on existing ones, even if they are opposed to them.
- Feminism challenged the male-centredness of a range of ideologies.
- Early or first-wave feminists challenged the exclusion of women from rights and citizenship.
- Second-wave feminism from the 1960s challenged the ways in which the public–private distinction had been understood, suggesting that 'the personal is political'.

7 POLITICAL THEORY AND IDEOLOGY: DIFFERENT BUT RELATED?

We have seen that normative political theory, on the one hand, and ideology, on the other, bring key political concepts together and provide them with certain, contested, meanings. This point in common also provides us with a useful way of separating political ideology from normative political theory. Both use the same raw materials of political concepts, and both derive their meaning from the historically and culturally specific conditions in which they are located. Nevertheless, there are important differences.

- Political theory uses specialist language which is often aimed at professional and specialist groups primarily in the academy, whereas political ideologies are constructed to generate mass or popular appeal.
- Political theory places a special emphasis on pinning down the precise meaning of concepts, whereas political ideologies are concerned less with precision and more with the impact of political ideas.
- Political theory produces 'tentative formulations' (provisional statements) that can be revised through dialogue and argument, whereas ideologies seek some degree of fixity and certainty in political beliefs.

With reference to the first difference, we need to take account of the fact that the division between the academy and wider political arena is increasingly blurred. Consider the increasing role of 'public intellectuals' (see Andrews' outline of the interventions of Scruton, Hayek and Giddens in Chapter 3) in articulating political theory in the context of policy communities and think-tanks. Even John Locke and John Stuart Mill, whose texts form the object of analysis for political theory, were writing as a contribution to the political system in which they lived. Locke sought to make a direct contribution to the debates in the 1680s on restraining the power of the absolutism of the crown and in developing ideas for a constitutional monarchy accountable to parliament that proved to be influential in the aftermath of the Glorious Revolution (see Chapter 1). Mill was concerned to promote specific conceptions of liberty, meritocracy and parliamentary reform in the 1850s and 1860s, serving as an MP from 1865 to 1868. So, political theorists may have interpreted the world but many of them have also sought to conserve, reform or (in the case of Marxist and feminist theorists) transform the society they inhabit.

Michael Freeden argues that the study of ideology is more than the public pronouncements of politicians and the written texts (articles, pamphlets and books) on what politics ought to be about. It involves the study of the conditions in which such interventions are made, the consequences of ideological projects and an awareness of the tacit assumptions of those involved (Freeden, 1996, pp.43–5). Ideas matter in two ways. First, political agents use ideas to define positions and set them apart from other agents. For example, leftist projects tend to emphasize egalitarianism and the greatest good for the greatest number. Rightist projects tend to combine trust in tradition with individual responsibility. But the ideas used are also contested in more fundamental ways. The meaning of a concept such as equality, justice, liberty or the individual depends on how it is used in the construction of a political discourse. *Concepts* such as freedom and liberty mean different things to a liberal compared with an anarchist or a socialist.

Furthermore, it is not just a matter of saying that each concept has a different definition depending on which political theory or ideology in which it is inserted, for concepts also have an internal complexity. Freeden argues that we should think of them as 'cluster concepts' made up of elements that have different purposes.

- *Ineliminable elements* are the core definitions that are central to the concept and which cannot be eliminated or it would not be the same concept.

- *Adjacent elements* clarify the precise use of the concept.

- *Peripheral elements* do not add definition but still help in making a concept relevant for the political practices in a specific time and place or in specific institutions.

Freeden uses a practical illustration of a table: the ineliminable element of a table is a 'flat raised surface' (without which it would not be a table). In the study of political concepts, 'liberty' has the ineliminable or core element of 'non-constraint' without which it would simply be a *different* concept.

To make sense of this object we also need to think in terms of the adjacent elements (such as kitchen table, dining table, meeting table) which clarify its purpose or use. These elements may be logically adjacent (self-development or self-determination are both logically adjacent alternatives for liberty). It is also difficult to make sense of liberty as self-determination without including other concepts in a logical relationship such as democracy or self-government.

Then there are culturally adjacent elements such as 'community'. These are shaped by the beliefs, values and institutions that have intellectual and emotional significance in a specific time and place and are used by the individuals, groups or movements involved.

Remember, the elements of concepts are not mutually exclusive. The ineliminable elements of one concept may also serve as adjacent and peripheral elements in another concept (the idea of a 'flat raised surface' may also serve as an adjacent element for a 'roof' or as a peripheral element of a 'garden patio'). Peripheral elements for the use of liberty may include 'natural rights' (though in another time and place, that of John Locke, it would have been at the core) or 'social order' (which in accounts of liberty is simply the by-product of voluntary associations between individuals). Other peripheral elements may not even be concepts but aphorisms (pithy communicative statements), which in the case of liberty could involve 'dog eat dog', 'charity begins at home' or 'you have no-one to blame but yourself'. These peripheral elements could be the primary way in which individuals express their ideological position. Studying ideology means focusing on the issues, policies, attitudes, 'facts' and practices in a specific time and place, for ideologies try to ensure that all the elements are defined, combined and arranged in such a way as to ensure that the concepts are *decontested*, that they appear to have some sort of fixity and certainty in a specific time and place (Freeden, 1996, pp.47–95).

Freeden suggests that if a concept is analogous to a table as a piece of furniture then we should see ideologies as a 'room', with each type of room usually involving certain kinds of furniture which often have some proximity to each other. Just as you would be surprised to see a toilet in a living room, it is hard to imagine conservative ideologies as having civil disobedience as an ineliminable or core element. Each component of a theory or ideology interacts with all the others and is changed when any one of the other components alters. This helps to explain how theories or ideologies are so varied and continually reinvented depending on the circumstances. Normative political theorists offer a kind of feng shui in the organization of the furniture, whereas the study of ideology is more interested in how the inhabitants live in the room. To illustrate the open-endedness and flexibility of ideologies the next section is devoted to ideological change in the UK in the second half of the twentieth century.

SUMMARY

- Rather than seeing them as separate activities, normative political theory is primarily concerned with clarifying ineliminable and adjacent concepts whereas the study of political ideologies has a greater focus on the use of concepts in specific contexts.
- Political concepts and ideas are always open to alternative definitions, and can be combined in different ways with other concepts and ideas.

8 POLITICAL IDEOLOGIES IN PRACTICE: THE EBB AND FLOW OF CONSENSUS AND CONFLICT

One of the distinctive features of politics has been the phases of contestation and consensus in political ideas. It has been suggested that the late twentieth century has produced a new era of ideological convergence, where the fundamentals, such as how to manage the economy, are not in question. It is useful to compare this with earlier periods of convergence and discord. During the 1950s there was remarkably common agreement on the role of the state in many Western societies. By way of illustration, both major political parties in the UK were committed to economic demand management, stable prices, full employment, welfare security (from the cradle to the grave) and nationalization as a strategy for safeguarding public utilities (the mixed economy).

They also agreed on the key principles of foreign policy (specifically the 'strong independent nuclear deterrent'). Areas of disagreement were confined to specific issues, such as education and housing. For example, there was sharp disagreement over the rights of tenants and the powers of landlords, as well as conflict on land-use and planning policy. The commitment to public provision of housing and education at a much higher level than any previous period was not in question. The question of what was the responsibility of the state or citizen still mattered in political rhetoric but not on the big issues of the day. Political theorists in the West responded to this state of affairs by proclaiming an 'end to ideology', while political scientists concentrated on describing smoothly functioning political systems.

By the 1980s there was no longer the same agreement on the role of the state nor on welfare provision. Contemporary political theorists talked of a resurgence of ideology and a resurrection of class conflict, while political scientists gathered evidence on the 'ungovernable' society. Focusing on the UK again, while Labour politicians retained a commitment to the social democratic consensus, conservative ideology had shifted towards what has become known as Thatcherism, a combination of conservative assumptions and freeing the individual by rolling back the frontiers of the state. This meant that many issues ('social problems') prompting state intervention before, such as poverty, homelessness and unemployment, were now portrayed as a matter of personal responsibility.

The ideological differences between left and right were reinforced by the Labour Party charting a national route to 'democratic socialism' with a clear commitment to an interventionist state, combined with withdrawal from the

European Community and unilateral nuclear disarmament. Labour also drew on the new social movements concerned with the environment, peace, women's rights, gay rights, the rights of disabled people and cultural difference. Neo-liberalism, in many ways the ideology behind Thatcherism, stressed the free market and property ownership, a strong version of self-reliant individualism, personal responsibility and the idea that some degree of social inequality was natural and acceptable. In the 1980s, ideological divisions were more evident than before, both between political parties and within them.

Ideologies do not actually disappear and pop up again; their advocates often work away on the fringes or as groupings within the parties. What we can conclude is that when comparing the 1920s–1930s as the 'age of ideologies', the late 1940s–1950s as the post-war (social democratic) consensus, and the resurgent ideologies of the 1960s–1980s, there are different kinds of ideological contestation taking place. What about the positions now in the UK? In order to capture the support necessary for forming an alternative government, the Labour Party was reinvented as 'new labour' in the 1990s (changing its assumptions, policies and even its political imagery from the iconic red flag to a red rose with a pinkish tint). Its departure from an ideological commitment to state intervention and collective ownership of the means of production shifted it away from being a strongly socialist party. The centre party, the Liberal Democrats, found themselves committed to political assumptions that were seen to be to the left of Labour.

FIGURE 5.5 Changing symbols as well as substance: the UK Labour Party moves from the 'by-hand-and-by-brain' badge from the 1950s to the contemporary red rose

New Labour's acceptance of many of the policies and institutional reforms of the Thatcher era could be said to represent a new 'neo-liberal consensus' (an agreement on the balance of state and economy). In the 'partnership' of public and private sectors (a new mixed economy) the state facilitates commercial and industrial development rather than being involved directly. More overt ideological conflict has again crystallized in certain narrow policy areas, with the sharpest disputes on the role of state and private sector in health and transport, although crime and justice policy (sometimes focused on asylum policy) is a close third.

Similar patterns of ideological reconfiguration have taken place in other Western societies, with a neo-liberal consensus acting as a centre of gravity within the diverse democratic systems in each case. With the collapse of communist states in Russia and Eastern Europe and economic reform of the People's Republic of China, US intellectuals have claimed that we have witnessed a new 'end of ideology'. Francis Fukuyama has described this as an 'end of history' (Fukuyama, 1992). This does not mean that history or social change has ended, but that the fundamental differences between those who see the future as capitalist or communist ('history with a capital H') have been resolved in favour of capitalist economics and liberal political institutions.

Just as the earlier idea of the end of ideology was mistaken (an inadequate way of characterizing a narrowing of ideological discourse), so too *The End of History* can be seen as simplistic and misleading. It ignores, for example, the proliferation of fundamentalist groups informed by various interpretations of Islam and Christianity. In addition, Peter Saunders (1995) argues that debates between capitalists and Marxists have been reinvented in the ideological projects defending transnational capitalism and free trade or attacking capitalism for causing environmental degradation, promoting global injustice (an accusation from the fair trade movement) and creating dangerous biotechnological risks.

SUMMARY

- Political ideas are always in competition and essentially contested, but the terms of debate shift in periods of consensus or discord in the manner of a concertina.

- Ideological projects (such as Thatcherism or New Labour) are hybrid combinations of concepts and assumptions from different ideological traditions seeking to control the political agenda.

- In periods of consensus, ideological projects are characterized by (in particular) agreement on the relationship between state and economy, but in periods of discord ideologies perform a transformative role around such issues.

9 RETHINKING IDEOLOGY AND THEORY

It is commonly assumed that political ideologies are coherent and self-referential bodies of thought based on foundational principles. There are some manifestations of political doctrines such as 'Marxism–Leninism' in the Soviet Union or National Socialism that were like this; however, even in these examples, contestation did take place and these doctrines evolved through complex debates within the narrow terms of reference permitted (such as between Trotskyism and Stalinism).

The very fact that these are exceptional forms of ideologies means that we need a flexible understanding of the concept of ideology that takes account of diverse agents, institutions and complex conditions. Similarly, as with the 'end of ideology' claim, the tendency to assume that ideologies are present only when there is significant political discord misses the way that discord operates under the surface of policy debates.

As I argued above, if we see theory as a toolbox, then perhaps we need a corresponding picture of ideologies as a kind of workbench. Ideologies involve the application of theoretical tools in order to have an effect on the actual conduct of politics. Earlier it was suggested that ideologies link political concepts, as analysed in political theory, and their political manifestations in institutions and policy-making communities. To take this further, we need to look at an example where established political ideas became questionable and new ideologies are forged. If we consider again how the social democratic consensus gave way to Thatcherism, we can see how ideologies can be understood as more malleable and flexible than is often assumed. The Keynesian welfare state was destabilized following a long period of economic stagflation. The emergence of alternative strategies on the left and the right for resolving the fiscal crisis of the state demonstrates the fragility of political ideologies.

The neo-liberal alternative sought to restore free market competition and deregulation, valuing free choice as beneficial for the society as well as the individual. But this neo-liberalism alone was not sufficient. Thatcherism had to be an ideological hybrid to mobilize conservatives motivated by the importance of family values, self-discipline, traditional education, law and order, and the fear of immigration (of 'being swamped'). Free collective bargaining, property ownership and lower income taxes were proposed in a populist appeal to individuals over the heads of their usual sectional interests, such as the trade unions. It was this unique combination that led one critic to coin the term 'Thatcherism' and define it as 'authoritarian populism' (Hall, 1980, p.1983).

In the previous sections we explored Freeden's analysis of the conceptual complexity of political theory and political ideologies (Freeden, 1996). When confronted with a hybrid phenomena such as 'Thatcherism' or 'authoritarian populism', we can begin to see the occasional limits of normative political theory. One task of normative political theory is to clarify the contradictions and confusions of such concrete ideological projects. But we also need a means of explaining how this ideological project managed to mobilize consent to outmanoeuvre its opponents, how it changed the ideological agenda and how it fared politically in the light of these elements. This is where the study of ideologies comes into its own. Freeden's analysis helps us understand how the Thatcherite project could draw out conceptual elements in existing ideologies (*disarticulation*) and rearrange them to provide a very different diagnosis of the society's problems (*rearticulation*) in a way that was directly relevant to groups in society that were unhappy with the current political situation.

In particular, the Thatcherite project focused on concepts such as state intervention and collectivism, disarticulating them from their associations with the benevolent paternal state looking after those unable to attain economic security. These concepts were rearticulated as a 'nanny state', an unwanted intrusion into the private lives of British people. The advocates of social democracy found that the more they emphasized the task of government as an agent of altruism and amelioration, the more they fell into the trap of being seen as statist, bureaucratic purveyors of creeping collectivism. In contrast, neo-liberals emphasized the virtues of individual choice, freedom and personal responsibility.

This example draws our attention to how political ideas can be disarticulated from an existing political ideology and rearticulated in a way that changes the political agenda. The immediate effect was to recast the electoral politics of the UK. The longer term result was that the left was unable to recapture the initiative until it, too, had radically re-thought its political vocabulary. The task of disarticulating the conceptual elements of Thatcherism, and rearticulating them in a way that built an alternative electoral coalition, was only completed in the 1990s with the emergence and election of New Labour. Indeed, the task was made easier for them because of the contradictory components of conservatism and neo-liberalism in Thatcherism. Tensions surfaced between individual freedom (in economic activity and property ownership) and social responsibility (preserving the values and moral fabric of the community). Some neo-liberals wanted to extend free choice to social issues such as sexual preference and drugs. New Labour secured a foothold in the ideological discourses by rearticulating the idea of social responsibility through a commitment to public services and rebuilding communities but, in the process, had to swallow most of the economic agenda of Thatcherism.

What can we conclude from this illustration? Ideologies are ongoing projects that can evolve or transform themselves fairly rapidly as political circumstances change. This means that, far from being dogmatically rigid belief systems, political ideologies are much more fragmentary; the ideas and concepts involved are open to disarticulation and rearticulation in a much more open way than is often assumed. Particular attention needs to be devoted to how such ideas as 'freedom' are defined and how the meaning of such ideas is dependent on how they combined with other ideas as part of a specific ideological project. If we take the workbench analogy seriously, we always need to situate the meaning of ideologies in terms of the concrete political practices through which they are reinforced and sometimes transformed. The most successful ideological projects draw together a range of social groups in order to provide intellectual and moral leadership in a given time and place, voicing the fears and concerns of these groups, expressing their material interests, and providing a framework within which these interests will be addressed. Moreover they have to tap into the rationalities of political culture which provide citizens with the capacity to make judgements on the right course of action and the desired outcome.

SUMMARY

- Political concepts are essentially contested and their meanings provisional; concepts or ideas such as legitimacy, self-determination, justice, freedom and equality derive meaning from how they are defined in relation to other concepts and how they are used in political practices.

- Political theory provides a toolbox for clarifying the meaning of concepts and ideas and helping us to establish which elements are core (ineliminable) and which are peripheral.

- The study of political ideologies provides a workbench on which the tools provided by political theory can cast light on the complex, changing and hybrid ideologies that are produced through the practical uses of concepts.

REFERENCES

de Beauvoir, S. (1972; first published 1949) *The Second Sex* (trans. Parshley, H.M.), Harmondsworth, Penguin.

Berlin, I. (1969) *Four Essays on Liberty*, Oxford, Oxford University Press.

Bond, R. and Saunders, P. (1999) 'Routes of success: influences on the occupational attainment of young British males', *British Journal of Sociology*, vol.50, no.2, pp.216–48.

Collins, P.H. (1990) *Black Feminist Thought: Knowledge, Politics and the Politics of Empowerment*, London, Routledge.

Freeden, M. (1996) *Ideologies and Political Theory*, Oxford, Oxford University Press.

Fukuyama, F. (1992) *The End of History and the Last Man*, New York, Free Press.

Gray, J. (1995) *Berlin*, London, HarperCollins/Fontana.

Hall, S. (1980) 'Popular-democratic vs. authoritarian populism: two ways of taking democracy seriously' in Hunt, A. (ed.) *Marxism and Democracy*, London, Lawrence and Wishart.

Hansard (2003) http://www.publications.parliament.uk/pa/cm200304/cmhansrd/vo031217/debtext/31217-03.htm (accessed December 2004).

Lemert, C. (ed.) (1993) *Social Theory: The Multicultural and Classic Readings*, Oxford, Westview.

Popper, K.R. (1945) *The Open Society and its Enemies*, London, Routledge.

Saunders, P. (1995) *Capitalism: A Social Audit*, Buckingham, Open University Press.

Scruton, R. (1984) *The Meaning of Conservatism* (2nd edn), Harmondsworth, Penguin.

Wollstonecraft, M. (1975; first published 1792) *A Vindication of the Rights of Women*, Harmondsworth, Penguin.

FURTHER READING

Berlin, I. (1969) 'Two concepts of liberty' in *Four Essays on Liberty*, Oxford, Oxford University Press.

Freeden, M. (1996) *Ideologies and Political Theory*, Oxford, Oxford University Press.

Gaus, G.F. and Kukathas, C. (eds) (2004) *Handbook of Political Theory*, London, Sage.

Goodin, R.E. and Pettit, P. (eds) (1993) *A Companion to Contemporary Political Philosophy*, Oxford, Blackwell.

Acknowledgements

Grateful acknowledgement is made to the following sources for permission to reproduce material in this book.

Chapter 1

Figures

Figure 1.1: © PA Photos; Figure 1.2: from Thomas Hobbes, 'Leviathan, or the Matter, Forme & Power of a Common-wealth, Ecclesiastical and Civil' © The British Library; Figure 1.3: © Time Life Pictures/Getty Images.

Cartoons

p.15: Centre for the Study of Cartoons and Caricature, University of Kent. © David Austin; p.16: Centre for the Study of Cartoons and Caricature, University of Kent. © John Jensen.

Chapter 2

Figures

Figure 2.1: © SIPA Press/Rex Features; Figure 2.2: © Empics Ltd; Figure 2.3 (left): © Israel Infotour; (right): © Jan de Jong; Figure 2.4: © Rafiqur Rahman/Reuters.

Cartoon

p.56: Centre for the Study of Cartoons and Caricature, University of Kent. © News International Syndication.

Chapter 3

Figures

Figure 3.1: © Melanie Stengal/Bettmann/CORBIS; Figure 3.2: © Eitan Abramovich/Getty Images; Figures 3.3 and 3.4: © Mary Evans Picture Library; Figure 3.5: © Adalberto Roque/Getty Images.

Cartoon

p.69: Centre for the Study of Cartoons and Caricature, University of Kent. © Mirrorpix.

Chapter 4

Figure 4.1: © Chris Keulen/Panos Pictures; Figure 4.2: © Jane Reed/Harvard News Office.

Cartoons

p.97: Centre for the Study of Cartoons and Caricature, University of Kent. © Dave Gaskill; p.110: P.J. Polyp. Originally printed in *New Internationalist* magazine, Issue 362, November 2003; p.113: P.J. Polyp. Originally printed in *New Internationalist* magazine, Issue 365, March 2004.

Chapter 5

Figures

Figure 5.1: © PA Photos; Figure 5.2: © Gregory Bull/Associated Press; Figure 5.3: © Steve Pyke; Figure 5.4: Copyright © Graphical, Paper and Media Union, by kind permission; Figure 5.5 (both): Courtesy of The People's History Museum.

Cover

Image copyright © PhotoDisc, Inc.

Index